To - Joe
12-25-07
Good Luck & Enjoy Life

Regards, Gord

Wounded At Gettysburg

A book of 44 letters written by a Civil War soldier to his family members

by

Gord Skinner

Bloomington, IN  Milton Keynes, UK

AuthorHouse™ *AuthorHouse*™ *UK Ltd.*
1663 Liberty Drive, Suite 200 *500 Avebury Boulevard*
Bloomington, IN 47403 *Central Milton Keynes, MK9 2BE*
www.authorhouse.com *www.authorhouse.co.uk*
Phone: 1-800-839-8640 *Phone: 08001974150*

©2007 Gord Skinner. All rights reserved.

No part of this book may be reproduced, stored in a retrieval system, or transmitted by any means without the written permission of the author.

First published by AuthorHouse 9/18/2007

ISBN: 978-1-4259-8253-9 (sc)

Printed in the United States of America
Bloomington, Indiana

This book is printed on acid-free paper.

Book recounts letters of local Civil War soldier

Sean Dobbin
Staff writer

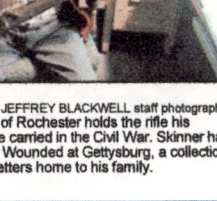

(November 11, 2007) — In August of 1862, William H. Skinner Jr. departed Rochester with the 108th Infantry to join the Union Army's 2nd Corps in the war against the Confederacy. For the next six years, he sent letters to his family, and a century later, his great-nephew Gordon Skinner started rounding them up.

In June, Skinner, 92, self-published *Wounded at Gettysburg*, a collection of 44 letters which chronicle the service of his great-uncle who was injured by an artillery shell in the Battle of Gettysburg.

"Forty years ago, I started collecting (the letters), bringing them in," says Skinner. "I made a loose-leaf notebook... but I never really thought of publishing it until the past year."

The 2nd Corps was one of the most heavily engaged units in the American Civil War. At Gettysburg, where William was injured, the 2nd Corps was the target of "Pickett's Charge," where the Confederacy attempted to break through the Union lines with a full frontal assault — an assault that ended in disaster for the Confederacy.

William's letters discuss topics ranging from battle experiences to 19th century medicine, and include anecdotes from day-to-day life.

Writes William on Feb. 25, 1863: "Our post happened to be just opposite the Reb's post on the other side of the river. ... One of them says, how did you like Fredericksburg and one of our boys says how did you like Antietam, and that is the way we keep it up."

Today, Skinner continues to make his home in Rochester, less than a mile from the area of his great-uncle's farm, which was near what is now Lake Avenue in the approximate area of the former Piehler Pontiac dealership. Along with his wife Helen, he has three daughters, eight grandchildren, and one great-grandchild.

Like his great-uncle, Skinner also served in the Army, spending four and a half years in an anti-tank outfit during World War II. During his service, his younger brother, who was a navigator in the Air Force, was shot down and killed over Austria. In U.S. military history, the Skinner name has popped up a number of times.

"If you go back far enough, one guy was in the Revolutionary War," says Skinner.

Upon returning from the Army, Skinner began a 32-year career at Kodak, where he developed a training program and worked as a technical writer. Skinner took an interest in hiking, becoming a "46er" by scaling the 46 tallest peaks in the Adirondacks.

When he finally decided to self-publish his great-uncle's letters, he chose the publisher AuthorHouse because it compared favorably to a few other publishing houses he found on the Internet.

"I get paid by the success of my authors," says Sean Stevens, Skinner's publishing consultant at AuthorHouse. "So it's a good motivation for me to help my authors become successful."

AuthorHouse is one of the few self-publishing companies that allows bookstores to return unsold books, which gives the stores added incentive to put AuthorHouse titles on their shelves. But so far, *Wounded at Gettysburg* is only available through the AuthorHouse Web site, or by special order in bookstores that work with AuthorHouse.

Skinner says he has tried to get the book into historical bookstores including the National Parks bookstore at Gettysburg, but has had trouble establishing contacts. Recently, he took out a $2,300 ad in *The New York Times*, hoping to spur sales.

"You gotta spend money to make money, but I hope I break even is all," says Skinner.

Skinner says that turning a profit was never his intention.

As he writes in his epilogue: "With the publication of this book a man's life is officially" laid to rest.

SDOBBIN@DemocratandChronicle.com

This book is dedicated to:

My wife ... Helen

My daughters ... Laurie
.... Sally
.... Penny

WOUNDED AT GETTYSBURG

... This book is a collection of 44 letters and other related information about my great uncle, William H. (Will) Skinner Jr., who was wounded in the Battle of Gettysburg July 3rd 1863.

... Will, the oldest son of William H. Skinner and Harriet C. Skinner, was born July 25, 1841.

... On August 8th 1862 Will was mustered in as a private in company F 108th Infantry at Rochester, N.Y. for a service of three years.

... Will was 21 years old, 5'9" tall, with light hair and complexion.

... His occupation was listed as a farmer on land known as "Hanford Landing" which is located between the Genesee River and Lake Avenue just east of Kodak Park.

... Will played the violin, liked music and was a good baseball player.

This book has been edited by Gord Skinner

Acknowledgements ... Special thanks to my cousins
Ellie Crumrine,
Jackie Fields,
Howie Newton
Carol Scheerens,
Sherry Tolle
Jean Wadsworth.

For the convenience of the reader of this book, the typed letters are typed with Will's original wording, spelling and punctuation.

Will Skinner, home on a furlough, displaying his wound on his **left thigh**.
This is a Tintype picture.
To properly view this picture look at it with a mirror.

William H. Skinner Jr. (Will)

b. July 25th 1841

d, Unknown

Will Skinner

at age 12 - 1852

Will Skinner wearing

Civil War uniform - 1862

Contents

Aug.	*1862*	*Letter to Mother from Arlington Heights, Va.*	2
Sept.	*1862*	*Letter to Mother, Father, Brothers, and Sisters*	4
Oct. 14,	*1862*	*Letter to Father from Harpers Ferry, Va.*	8
Dec. 4,	*1862*	*Letter to Mother from Camp in the Pine Woods*	12
Aug. to Dec.	*1862*	*Company Muster Roll & Regimental Description*	16
Jan. 24,	*1863*	*Letter to sister from Camp in the Woods*	18
Feb. 6,	*1863*	*Letter to Lucy from Camp near Falmouth, Va.*	22
Feb. 25,	*1863*	*Letter to Father from Camp in the Wilderness*	24
Mar. 14,	*1863*	*Letter to Hattie from Camp near Falmouth, Va.*	30
May 19,	*1863*	*Letter to Sister from Camp of the 108th Regiment*	32
June 12,	*1863*	*Letter to Mother from Camp near Falmouth, Va*	36
June 21,	*1863*	*Letter to Mother from Bull Run*	38
Aug. 1,	*1863*	*Letter to Hattie from Jarvis Hospital*	44
Aug. 9,	*1863*	*Letter to Lucy from Jarvis Hospital*	48
Aug. 12,	*1863*	*Letter to Hattie from Jarvis Hospital*	50
Aug.	*1863*	*Letter to Mother from Camp Palmer Washington, D.C.*	52
Sept. 8,	*1863*	*Letter to Lucy from Jarvis Hospital*	54
Sept. 28,	*1863*	*Letter to Sister from Jarvis Hospital*	56
Sept. & Oct.	*1863*	*Company Muster Roll & Hospital Muster Roll*	59
Nov. 19,	*1863*	*Letter to Sister from Jarvis Hospital*	62
Nov. 22,	*1863*	*Letter to Lucy from Jarvis Hospital*	66
Dec. 11,	*1863*	*Letter to Father from Jarvis Hospital*	67
Jan. 15,	*1864*	*Letter to Sister from Jarvis Hospital*	68
Jan. & Feb.	*1864*	*Company Muster Roll & Hospital Muster Roll*	70
Mar. 2,	*1864*	*Requisition for Transport of U.S. Troops*	71
Mar. 25,	*1864*	*Letter to Mother from Jarvis Hospital*	72
April 1,	*1864*	*Letter to Mother from Jarvis Hospital*	76
April 11,	*1864*	*Letter to Sister from Jarvis Hospital*	78
April 20,	*1864*	*Letter to George from Jarvis Hospital*	82

April 28,	*1864*	*Letter to Hattie from Jarvis Hospital*	*86*
May 8,	*1864*	*Letter to Hattie from Jarvis Hospital*	*88*
May 12,	*1864*	*Letter to George from Jarvis Hospital*	*92*
May 26,	*1864*	*Letter to Hattie from Jarvis Hospital*	*100*
June 15,	*1864*	*Letter to Sister from Jarvis Hospital*	*104*
June 20,	*1864*	*Letter to Mother from Camp Distribution*	*106*
July 23,	*1864*	*Letter to Mother from Camp 108th N.Y.V.*	*108*
Aug. 28,	*1864*	*Letter to Hattie from City Point Hospital*	*112*
Sept. 17,	*1864*	*Letter to Mother from Douglas Hospital*	*116*
Oct. 6,	*1864*	*Letter to Hattie from Douglas Hospital*	*120*
Oct. 21,	*1864*	*Letter to Lucy from Douglas Hospital*	*124*
Sept. & Oct.	*1864*	*Company Muster Roll & Hospital Muster Roll*	*129*
Nov. 4,	*1864*	*Fulough permit (To Whom It May Concern)*	*130*
Dec. 18,	*1864*	*Letter to Mother From Douglas Hospital*	*132*
Nov. & Dec.	*1864*	*Regimental Return, Company Muster Roll & Hospital Muster Roll*	*137*
Jan. 1,	*1865*	*Letter to Mother from Douglas Hospital*	*138*
Mar. 28,	*1865*	*Letter to Lucy from Douglas Hospital*	*142*
April 10,	*1865*	*Letter to Mother from Douglas Hospital*	*144*
April 20,	*1865*	*Letter to Lucy from Douglas Hospital*	*148*
May 4,	*1865*	*Letter to Hattie from Douglas Hospital*	*150*
May 28,	*1865*	*Company Muster Roll*	*155*
June 11,	*1865*	*Letter to Hattie from Douglas Hospital*	*156*
Jan. 20,	*1866*	*Application for Invalid Pension*	*160*
Feb. 10,	*1866*	*Pension Request*	*162*
Feb. 9,	*1866*	*Examining Surgeon's Certificate*	*164*
April 13,	*1867*	*Rejected ... Alleged disability does not exist*	*167*
Jan. 29,	*1868*	*Letter to Lucy from Manistee*	*168*
		Epilogue	*173*

Letter to Mother ... Letter has no date but the subject and timing of the letter suggests it was written in August 1862.

Dear Mother, We are now in Washington or very near it for we are on Arlington Heights where we have a good view of it. We had a good time coming but I believe there was one man killed in Rochester. I never felt better in my life than I do now. I have not much time to write fore we are busy. I saw Father in New York on Friday and he said I done just right. Tell Mary Jane I will write to her in a few days just as soon as I get a chance. You want to direct to Co. F 108 reg. NYU Arlington Heights, Virginia. Father said he was going home in a few days. Give my love to all the folks.

Your Son
W H Skinner

Dear Mother. We are now in washington or very near it for we are on Arlington heights where we have a good view of it We had a good time coming but I believe there was one man killed in Rochester. I never felt better in my life than I do now. I have not much time to write for we are busy I saw Father in New York on Friday and he said I done just right. Tell Mary Jane, I will write to her in a few days just as soon as I get a chance You want to direct to Co. F 108 reg. N.Y.V. Arlington Heights Virginia. Father said he was going home in a few days. I give my love to all the folks
Your son
W. H. Skinner

Letter to Mother, Father, Brothers & Sisters,

The subject matter suggests that it was written in September 1862 soon after the battle of Antietam.

Dear Mother, Father, Brothers & Sisters

I have just got time to write a few lines to you for I expect to be on the move again pretty soon. I know now what a battle is and its a glorious thing with balls banging around your head & men yelling and singing around you with a constant roar of musketry about you for _____ those are _____ were for it than if it was corn popping. We were in the front of the fight and the way we tumbled them over was a caution to white folks. You had ought to have seen our Captain (Pierce) wave his sward and call his men on. You will get the news in the paper better than I can write it. Jim Bowman is all right. I could tell you all that I would like to but I aint got time. Tell Mary Jane to write & not

Dear Mother & Father brothers & sisters,
I have just got time to write a few lines to you
the great battle is over again Mr. Brown, I know
he can't fear to write to you again luck to you, I know
was into a battle, and if a glorious one it was
Sally, I am sound and well — Sherman is bugeying around
giving [them?] a constant roar of musketry about you, I—
[illegible] it was over for But we are ready for a fresh
one if it were over tomorrow, We were in the front of the fight
and the many [illegible] lumber thrown over was a caution to us
But you [illegible] I ought to of seen our Captain (Price) wave his
cap and call his men on, You would get the news in the
papers better than I can write it. Jim Burmen is all
right a great of our delegation and that I would like
to tell you but I can't get time have Mary Jane to write if not

Letter to Mother, Father, Brothers & Sisters

to be mad because I don't. I may not have a chance to write again in a good while but I would like to have somebody from home write me. Please to hand the enclosed to Mary. Ask Joe Roworth if he ever was in battle all day, and on picket all night with the cusses pecking at you every chance they get. Give my respects to Mrs. Roworth and every body else. Get a side of beef and give it to Curlo. Did you get that check cashed without any trouble? Direct the same as the last and they will be forwarded to us here. I can't write any more for I had to beg to get this piece of paper.   from your son

W H Skinner

be glad to receive I don't I may not have a chance to write again in a good while but I would like to have somebody from home write to me. Please to hand the enclosed to Mary. Ask Joe Roworth if he ever was in battle all day and on picket all night with the crosses pocking at you every chance give any respects to John Roworth and every body else. yet a side of beef and give it to Cut did you get that check cashed without any trouble direct the same as the last and they will be forwarded to us There I cant write any more for I had to beg to get this piece of paper from you for

G. W. Kinnear

Letter to Father ... October 14th 1862

Harpers Ferry Oct. 14th 1862

Dear Father
The reason I had not written to you before was because I thought you was going home all the time. I did not want to send to N.Y. unless you was there but mother told me in her letter that I got yesterday that you was not home yet. I think if you can go home now it would be best for the crops want tending besides the the mare is sick & the Doctor tending her. Father, I want to ask your forgiveness for my conduct towards you, for I was a great deal to blame. I know I was very headstrong. I did not do right I know your feelings were toward me & if you can forgive me & look over it all I will be contented for we may never see each other again. I have sent several letters home & received several. Tom Smith reported around that Jim Bowman was sick in the hospital but it is not so. He stands it pretty well considering the state of his health when he left. I suppose you heard of the Battle we were in the 17th of September. It was pretty sharp work for four hours & a half, a continual roar of cannon & musketry. One of our generals rode up in front and shouted 108th your place is in the front & away went our

Harpers Ferry Oct. 14th 1862

Dear Father,

The reason I have not written to you before was because I thought you was going home all the time. I did not want to send to N.Y. unless you was there, but Mother told me in her letter that I got yesterday that you was not home yet. I think if you can go home now it would be best for the crops want tending, besides the mare is sick & the Docter tending her.

Father, I want to ask your forgiveness for my conduct towards you, for I know I was a great deal to blame. I know it was very headstrong. I did not do right. I know what your feelings were toward me & if you can forgive me & look over it all I will be contented for we may never see each other again. I have sent several letters home, & received several.

Tom Smith reported around that Jim Bowen was sick in the Hospital but it is not so. He stands it pretty well considering the state of his health where he left. I suppose you heard of the Battle we were in the 17th of September, it was pretty sharp work for four hours & a half, a continual roar of cannon & musketry. One of our generals rode up in front and shouted 108th your place is in the front, & away went our

Letter to Father ... October 14th 1862

blankets & haversacks & into it we went, load and fire as fast as we could, the reb's were about eight rods from us in a corn field. I went over the field a couple of days after & it was an awful sight they were piled one on the other just as they stood in the ranks. Gen. McClellan gave us praise for conduct as green troops. The way the balls & buckshot whistled around our ears was a caution, but after we fired two or three times we did not mind it, the shells whizzing & bursting around us, men yelling & jackasses braying it was considerable of a concert. Give my respects to Offerman & all the rest of the engineering friends & please answer this. Send me the news direct to Co. F 108 Reg. Washington, D.C. We are camped at Harpers Ferry. I guess we will stay here all winter.

From your son
W. H. Skinner

Blankets & Haversacks & into it we went had & fire as fast as we could, the reb's were about eight rods from us in a corn field. & went over the field a couple of days after, & it was an awful sight they were piled one on the other just they stood in the ranks Gen. McClellan gave us praise for conduct as green troops; the way the balls & buckshot whistled around our ears was a caution, but after we fired two or three times we did not mind it, the shells whizzing & bursting around us, men yelling & Jackasses braying it was considerable of a concert. Give my respects to Offerman & all the rest of engineering friends & please answer this & send me the news. Direct to Co. F. 108 Reg Washington D.C. We are camped at Harpers Ferry & I guess we will stay here all winter

From your Son

W. H. Skinner

Letter to Mother ... December 4th 1862

Camp in the Pine Woods   Dec. 4th 1862

Dear Mother, I hope you have not worried yourself on my account, for I am as well and feel just the same as I always have. Well, we were sent to Ball Plaines on detached duty some time ago, that is to repair roads & such like jobs in stead of marching all over this God forsaken country but we shoulder our guns and strap on our knapsacks and marched out to where our work lay as it was too far to walk every morning and night. The weather is beautiful here nice and worm in the day, and just cool enough in the night so that one blanket over us is enough and but very little rain. We have lots of rations as well and good ones too. I have forgotten one thing. I wish if you have any of those heart cases about the house yet you would let one of the girls fix up five or six of them with tape, you know how I mean, for they are just what I want to put coffee, sugar, rice beans and other little things in and roll up a couple in a paper and send me and put the rest in the box if it aint too late. They have a dried vegetables and it is nice to put in soup. It swells up & is almost as good as if they were green. This is the last piece of paper I can scare up and I have got to beg a stamp.

Camp in the pine woods, Dec 4th 1862

Dear Mother, I hope you have not worried yourself on my account, for I am as well and feel just the same as I always have. Well, we were sent to Bell Plains on Detached duty some time ago, that is to repair roads & such like jobs, instead of marching all over this God forsaken country, but we shouldered our guns and strapped on our knapsacks and marched out to where our work lay, as it was too far to walk every morning and night. The weather is beautiful here, nice and warm in the day, and just cool enough in the night so that one blanket over us is enough, and but very little rain. We have lots of rations as well, and good ones too. I have forgotten one thing. I wish if you have any of those heart cases about the house yet you would let one of the girls fix up five or six of them with tape on your knap—— I mean, for they are just what I want to put coffee, sugar, rice, beans and other little things in, and roll up a couple in paper and send me, and put the rest in the box if it ain't too late. They have a new ration they give us lately, it is dried vegetables, and it is nice to put in soup, it swells up & it almost is good as if they were green. This is the last piece of paper I can scare up and I have got to beg a stamp, an

Letter to Mother ... December 4th 1862

so you had better make up a bundle of paper envelopes & stamps & send me. We get our rations of whisky now nearly every night but we have the greatest times for tobacco. Our butler can't get his goods and the boys are all grumbling because they can't get any tobacco and if one happens to have some he will trade it for anything and he will take a chew then trade it to somebody else and it will go from one to another. There my beets are almost boiled dry and I must pour some more water on the them for my dinner and I guess I will have some rice and molasses & a cup of coffee for supper, we have everything handy here, we are camped in the woods & a stream of nice clear water close by. Now this is what I call pleasant. The sun shinning down nice and warm with our dinners cooking & one of the best Captains that ever commanded a company to make things go off nice. Has father come home yet? I sent him a letter & until he answers that I will write no more for if he will not answer it I will know the reason very well. Well I can't think of anything more at present. Give my love to all the family. Oh I guess Jim will be home shortly.

From your son
W H Skinner

So you had better make up a bundle of paper envelopes & stamps & send me. We get our rations of whiskey now nearly every night. but we have the greatest times for tobacco, our sutler cant get his goods here and the boys are all grumbling because they can't get any tobacco and if one happens to have some he will trade it for something and he will take a chew and then trade it to somebody else and so it will go from one to another. There my beans are almost boiled dry and I must put some more water on them for my dinner and I guess I will have some rice and molases & a cup of coffee for supper, we have every thing handy here, we are camped in the woods & a stream of nice clear water close by. Now this is what I call pleasant, the sun shining down nice and warm with our dinners cooking & one of the best Captains that ever commanded a company to make things go off nice. Has Father came home yet. I sent him a letter & untill he answers that I will write no more for if he will not answer it I will know the reason very well. Well I cant think of any thing more at present. Give my love to all the family. Oh I guess Jim will be home in

From your Son

| S | 108 | N.Y. |

Wm Skinner
Pvt., Co. F, 108 Reg't N. Y. Infantry.

Appears on

Company Muster Roll

for Aug. 31 to Dec. 31, 1862.

Present or absent Present.

Stoppage, $ _____ 100 for _____

Due Gov't, $ _____ 100 for _____

Remarks: _____

Book mark: _____

Cobb

| S | 108 | N.Y. |

William Skinner
_____, Co. F, 108 Reg't N. Y. Infantry.

Appears on

Regimental Descriptive Book

of the regiment named above.

DESCRIPTION.

Age 21 years; height 5 feet 9 inches.
Complexion light
Eyes gray; hair light
Where born New York, New York
Occupation farmer

ENLISTMENT.

When Aug. 8, 1862.
Where Rochester
By whom F. E. Pierce; term 3 y'rs.
Remarks: _____

Hammond

Father - Wm H. Skinner Sr.

b. December 22nd 1810 in Albany, N.Y.
d. July 31st 1869 in Rochester, N.Y.

Mother - Harriet C. Skinner

b. 1818 in New York City
d. July 4th 1872 in Rochester, N.Y.

Letter to Sister ... January 24th 1863

Camp in the Woods   Jan. 24, 1863

Dear Sister   I received your letter yesterday morning with one dollar but the one with one and a half I have not got yet but there is one thing I have got though and that is a felon on my first finger on my right hand. So I must scribble with my left but I guess you will manage to read it after a fashion. Tell Jim I got his letter but have not been able to write for want of stamps. I will answer his and all the rest as soon as my hand gets well.. Tell him to write me and give me all the news. I suppose he is getting well as you don't say any different. I don't remember telling Jim Rigny not to write. Tell him I would be glad to hear from him and all the boys. I saw Clem Olmsted and took a walk with him a few days ago and I saw John Dean and Ambrose Langworthy and Teen. And I saw Gus Hall once. I wish you had sent about 4 pounds of tobacco in that letter instead of a chew. I expect that box every day. If you see Louisa tell her I got her letter but could not answer it but I will as soon as I can. We have fine

Camp in the woods Jan 24, 1863

Dear Sister, I received your letter yesterday morning with one dollar, but the one with one and a half I have not got yet, but there is one thing I have got though and that is a felon on my first finger of my right hand. So I must scribble with my left, but I guess you will manage to read it after a fashion. Tell Jim I got his letter but have not been able to write for the want of stamps. I will answer his and all the rest as soon as my hand gets well. Tell him to write to me and give me all the news. I suppose he is getting well as you don't say any different. I don't remember telling Jim Rigny not to write, tell him I would be glad to hear from him and all the boys. I saw Chan Olmsted and took a walk with him a few days ago, and I saw John Dean and Ambrose Langworthy and F Teen. And I saw Jus Hall once. I wrote you had sent about 4 pounds of tobacco in that letter instead of a chew. I expect that box every day. If you see Louisa tell her I got her letter but could answer it but I will as soon as I can. We have fine

Letter to Sister ... January 24th 1863

times now getting wood we only have to go just out side our kennel and waddle about two miles through mud and slush up to our ankles. But that is nothing to picking cherries. Tell mother I borrowed two dollars of Jim Bowman and I would like to have her pay it to him. I would like to have seen those photographs tell DeWitt to go and pull all the wagons and things to pieces. I won't scold him. Give my love to mother and all the rest.

From your brother   W H Skinner

times now getting wood. we only have
to go just outside of our Kennel and
waddle about two miles through
mud and slush up to our ankles
but that is nothing to picking cherries
Tell Mother I borrowed two dollars
of Jim Bowman and I would
like to have her pay it to him.
I would like to seen those
photographs tell Jewett to go
and pull all the wagons and things
to pieces I won't scold him. Give my
love to mother and all the rest
From your Brother W H L Skinner

Letter to Lucy ... February 6th 1863   **No original letter**

Dear Sister, I received your letter three or four days ago but my finger has not been well enough so I could write. If the folks there don't write oftener than they have lately I shall quit writing. I only had four letters and one paper in over a month and only one of them from home. Every other boy has lots of letters and papers to read. I wish you would send me the Mercury every week. It will only cost four cents a week and I want something to read to pass away the time these wet miserable days for it has been raining and snowing and freezing & blowing & thawing and raining & haling & pelting away at us here for the last three or four weeks so that we have to stay in our holes most of the time and amuse ourselves with a pack of cards or drilling a hole into a hard tack. We have all been paid off up to the first of January but I won't risk sending it home now. If you write to mother give her my love and tell her to remember me to the girls there. If I had known how to direct I should of written Emma Robertson & the rest of the folks there before this time for I should like to hear from them.

I have written to Mary Jane and several others there and got no answers from them so I shall quit. I sent you a letter a couple of days after the battle of Fredericksburg with another letter enclosed that came out of a reb's breast pocket for you to puzzle over but you haven't said anything about it. I believe I told you in one letter to send me a list of everything in the box but you haven't done it. I wish you would in the next letter you write tell me everything that was put in the box. If anything is taken out I can get it again.

How does DeWitt, George and Martha get along? It is very curious that Father don't write. I don't know what to make of it. I expect Jim is on his way here by this time by what you said so there is no use of my writing to him now. Well I must quit now. Give my respects to all the folks.

                                       Your Brother   *W. H. Skinner*

Letter to Father ... February 25th 1863

Comments are undoubtedly about the Battle of Fredricksburg

Camp in the Wilderness Feb. 25, 1863

Dear Father,

The girls say you have not received my letter. I thought it was strange you did not answer it but _____ with the mails lately, so it _____ _____ accounted for. Well I suppose you read all the war news, so on that respect I can't give you much information, unless it be some little incidents that transpires here once in a while. Last Friday morning at daylight they drummed us out _____ _____ on picket. We took up our positions at the _____ before the battle. When it came my squads turn to _____ we _____ _____ our post happened to be just opposite the Reb's post on the other side of the river. If I had a N.Y. or Rr. paper with me then I would of given a dollar, you see the boys on both sides are very talkative, so we talk to one another as handy as need be, as we are only about twice the with of the Genesee apart. As soon as they saw we were posting a new relief they thought they would open on us. One of them wanted to come across and give us southern news in exchange for one of our papers but none of us had one with us. One of them says, how did you like Fredericksburg and one of our boys says how did you like Antietam, and that is the way we keep it up. They want to know how we left the girls at home and why we didn't bring our Mother along.

Camp in the Wilderness ——

Dear Fath——

The Girls say that you have not
received my letter; I thought it was
strange since did not answer it but
with the mails lately, so it is all
accaunted for. Well, I suppose you
read all the war news, so in that
respect I can't give you much information, unless it be some little
incidents that transpire here once
in a while. Last friday morning
at daylight this day ————
out ————
a picket ————
at the ————
battle. When it comes my
turn to ————

our post happened to be just opposite
the Reb's post on 'tother side of the
river. If I had of had a N.Y. or Ph.
paper with me then I would of given
a dollar; you see the boys on both sides
are very talkative, so we talk to one
another as handy as need be, as we
are only about twice the width of
the Genesee apart. As soon as they
saw we were posting a new relief
they thought they would open on us
One of them wanted to come across
and give us southern news too in
exchange for one of our papers; but
none of us had one with us. One
of them says, how did you like Fredericksburg. And one of our boys says
how did you like Antietam, and
that is the way we keep it up.
They want to know how we left
the Girls at home, and why we
didn't bring our Mother along.

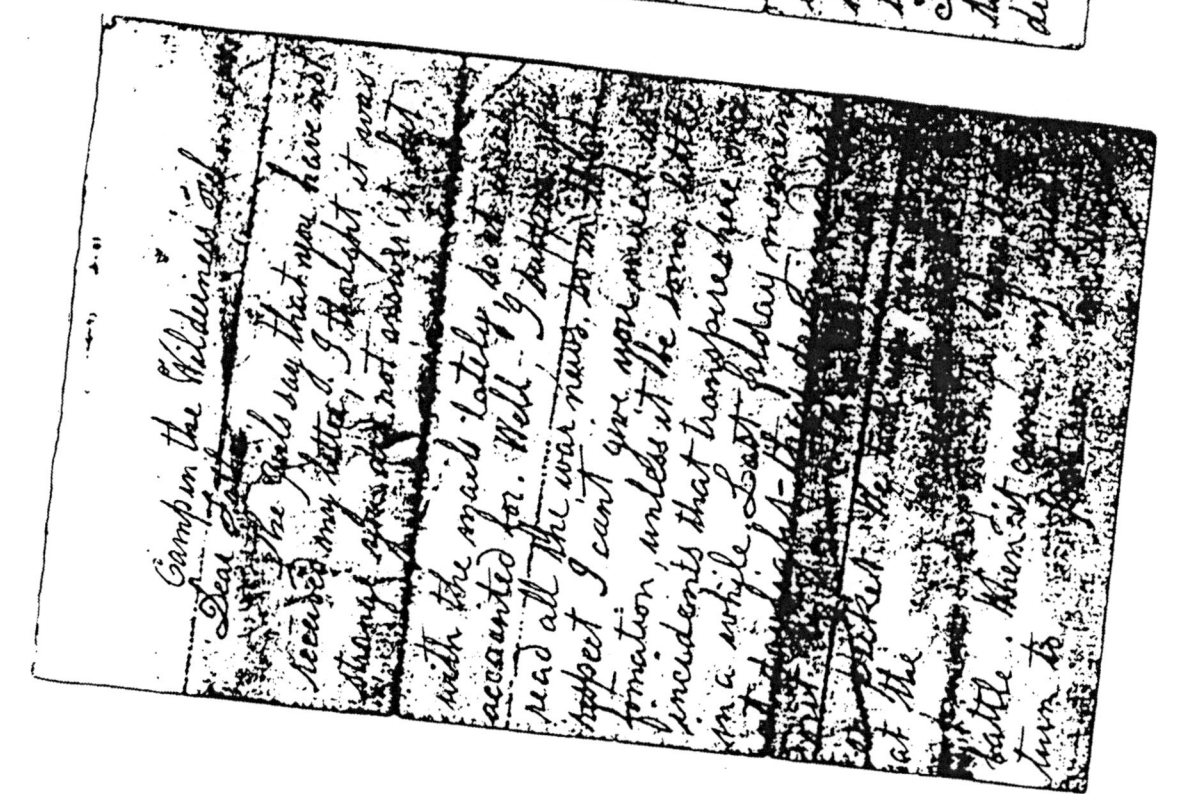

Letter to Father ... February 25th 1863

I suppose you heard that F. Dowin had his leg shot off. One of the boys in our company had his leg taken off while we were lying in front of a church. It fell about six feet from where I was sitting on the curbstone. It wounded four of our boys and covered many another young fellow and myself with mud. One piece of it (Oh I forgot to say it was a shell) splintered the curbstone between my feet. But I got a closer shave than that on the field for one of thier musket balls went through my coat just on top of my shoulder. I hear they are going to make a draft for 300,000 more men. I wonder what success they will have. Did you ever hear tell of a greyback? There is a couple running a race down my leg now and I guess one of them goes on crutches by the way he hop skips and jumps it. We have various ways of amusement down here; when it is fine weather we play ball, and when it is like it is now we snowball, for there was about a foot of snow fell Saturday night. Since Hooker has been in command we have lived on top shelf & the boys are afraid that he will resign. How is Mr. Offerman, Mr. Boughten and all the rest of N.Y. Give my respects to them all and if any of the Femermines inquire for me, please give them a few. I would like to of sent home a pair of silver goblets that I got in Fed. before the

I suppose you have heard that I Doggin had his leg shot off. One of the boys in our company that has his leg taken off while we were lying in front of a church. It fell about six feet from where I was sitting on the curbstone. It wounded four of our boys and comed another company colors to fell with mud & old pieces of shell. Oh I forgot to say it was a shell splintered the curbstone too. But I got a close shave that that on the field. One of their musket balls went through my coat just on top of my shoulder. I thew that it that was going to make a draft for 300,000 more men. I wonder what success they will have. Did you ever hear tell of a Greyback? There is a couple running a race down my leg now, and I guess one of them goes on

crutches by the way he skips & jumps it. I. We have various ways of amusement down here. When it is fine weather we play ball, and when it is likely it is now we throw ball for there was about a foot of snow fell that muddy night. Since Hooker has taken in command we have lived on the top shelf. The boys are afraid that he will resign. How is Mrs. Offerman, Mr. Boughten and all the rest of N.Y. Give my respects to them all and if any of the tenements enquire for me please give them a few. I would like to be at home a pare of hours I bet that I got on that in Fred before the

Letter to Father ... February 25th 1863

battle but it was impossible for we had so much other stuff to carry. As it was I managed to carry tobacco enough to last me till the present time and a little left yet; but the mugs were so large, they would hold a quart, that I could not carry them. They were solid silver and handsomely finished. But the way we pitched into pancakes and honey and everything else to be found in a large city was a caution. But all things must have an end. So away we start at the sound of the bugle, and into the fight, but it was no use, they had us in the trap, & the way they scattered men & horses around was curious, and they yelling to us, run you Yankee sons - - - - run, and all we could do was pull one side of us out of the mud and stick the others fast, and in that style get out of it the best was we could. As I have just one stamp which Hattie sent me, it will be the last letter that I can write until I can get some for they are a scarce article in this part of the country. If you see Phil & John Kirby, tell them to write to me, & tell all the rest too, for it is a treat to get a letter or any other news. Please answer this right away and tell me all the news. Direct WHS Co. F 108 Reg. N.Y. Wash. D.C. My love to you and mother & my respects to all the rest.

from your son.   *W. H. Skinner*

us, run your Yankee sons --- sun, and all we could do was pull one side of us out of the mud and stick the other fast, and in that style of it the best way we could. So I have just one stamp, Arthur Hoattie sent me in the last letter that I think will be the last letter that I write till I get some. I thank they are a scarse article in this part of the country — say Pap & John Zigler tell them to write to me. Tell all the rest too, for it is a treat to get a letter or any other news. Please answer this right away and tell me the news about Co I, 108 Rgt NSM. Hash DC—my love to you and Mother & my respects to all the rest — From your son, J. H. Shannon

battle, but it was impossible. We had so much other stuff to carry, as it was I managed to carry tobacco enough to last me till the present time and a little left yet, but the boys were so bad, they would take grant, that I could not carry them. Then were found silver and handsomely furnished. But the way we pitched into pan cakes and honey, and every thing else to be found was a large sity, away a can— But all things must have an end, so we soon made tracks at the high, but it was no use, they had us in the tight, & the way they scattered men & horses around was curious, and they felling to

Letter to Hattie ... March 14th 1863

Camp near Falmouth, March 14, 63

Dear Sister, I am going to send a few lines in John's letter and it must due for you and the rest of the family as I have no stamps. I cannot answer your letters so you must send me some or I can't write. You may tell the boys & girls there all of them that as they don't feel inclined to answer my letters. I will quit writing all together, except to answer letters that I receive from home & none else & if you do not furnish me with stamps I can't do that. You may tell them all that I have got tired of writing for nothing especially to those I was anxious to hear from. I expect we will have a battle soon & I hope we will for then I may forget that any _____ & would write & that others have forgotten me. But I my tell you all some day. Tell Lucy I can't write to her till you send me some stamps. I wrote to Father two weeks ago but he don't answer. Good bye for a while. The mail comes every day & all the boys but me are getting letters & papers & books to read while I have none. I am most tired of it. Give my love to Mother & all the rest of the family.

Your brother
W. H. Skinner

Seeing that John forgot to put this in I will send it myself and try it without a postage stamp. Tell Mary I thank her for those stockings & also James Rigney & tell Ben Allen those cigars are the best I have seen in this country.

Camp near Falmouth March 14. 63

Dear Julia

I am going to drop a few lines in John's letter & I guess I will do it and the rest of the family, as I have no stamps. I cannot answer your letters to any mind. some time or I can't write. You may tell the Boyer Girls that all of them that I think don't feel inclined to answer my letters I shall quit writing altogether except to answer letters that I receive from home. I never ans else, & if you do not punish me with stamps I can jist do that & you may tell them all that I have got tired of writing for nothing except to those I was anxious to hear from. I expect we will have a battle soon & I hope we will for three I may forget that Any write, & that others have forgotten me—But I may tell you all some day. Tell Lucy I can't write to her till you send me some stamps. I wrote to Father two weeks ago but they dont answer. Good by to a while & the mail comes every day & all the boys but me are

getting letters & papers and books read a while I have none. I am most tired of it. Give my love to mother & all the rest of the family.

Your Brother
W. H. Skinner

Seeing that John forgot to put this in I will send it by itself and try if nothing printed on. Tell Algert I thank & bittage stamps Tell Aggie & Annie tis for those stockings. Tell Allen those Cigars Bughey. I tell Ben I have been in this country are the best I have seen in this country—

Hattie E. Skinner

Letter to Sister ... May 19th 1863

Camp of the 108th Regt.
May 19th 1863

Dear Sister, I received your letter yesterday. I have written two or three letters since we had the fight; It's damming that none of them have reached you, I sent a twenty dollar bill in one of them and if that is lost I shall send no more for I had rather use it here than send it by mail and lose it. I do not remember how much plowing it was that I done for Keehl, but I am certain it is down in the book somewhere; and if I owe him for a pair of boots it must be two or three years ago; for the last pair I got

Camp of the 108th Regt.
May 19th 1863

Dear Sister. I received your letter yesterday. I have written two or three letters since we had the fight; it's ~~strange that~~ none ~~of them have reached you~~, I sent a twenty dollar bill in one of them and if that is lost I shall send no more for I had rather use it here than send it by mail and lose it. I do not remember how much ploughing it was that I done for Keahl but I am certain it is down in the book somewhere; and if I owe him for a pair of boots it must be two or three years ago; for the last pair I got

Letter to Sister ... May 19th 1863

before those you had sent me I bought in Rochester. If you look over it close I think you will find it. If that money reaches home, I wish you would take a couple of dollars of it and buy me a black neck handkerchief. Just fold it good in a paper and send it. to me. Has Jim Bowman got back to the Landing yet; give my respects to Bill Canolle, and tell him I will answer all letters he will send me. We have been moving camp since the fight We are now in a beautiful pine grove, with wood and water right under our nose, and a pretty good prospect of staying here for some time. It may be a month, and it may be three; but be it what it will, we could not have a pleasanter spot. We have preaching every sunday afternoon, and prayer meetings once or twice a week now, since we have had our present Chaplain We have also close by to us three bands, so we have plenty of music all the time. I have just come off picket on the banks of the Rappahannock. Give my respects to all the enquiring friends.

From your brother
W. H Skinner

before those you sent me. I bought in Rochester. If you took over it else I think you will find it. If that money reaches home, I wish you would take a couple of dollars of it and buy me a black neck handkerchief just fold it good in a paper and send it to me. has Jim Bousman got back to the Boarding yet. give my respects to Bill Sawold, and tell him I will answer all letters he will send me. We have been moving camp since the fight we are now in a beautiful pine grove, with wood and water right under our nose, and a pretty good prospect of staying here for some time.

It may be a month and it may be three; but be it what it will, we could not have a pleasanter spot. We have preaching every Sunday afternoon, and prayer meetings once or twice a week now, since we have had our present Chaplain. We lay also close by to us three bands, so we have plenty of music all the time. I have just come off picket on the Banks of the Rappahannock. Give my respects to all the enquiring friends. From your Brother
W H C Skinner

Letter to Mother ... June 12th 1863

Camp near Falmouth   *June 12th 1863*

Dear Mother I have received the girls letters all of them, and the papers that have been sent, also the handkerchief and hat. I was glad to get the hat for I was going to buy one. I hope you will continue to send me those papers. I also got Hatties Photograph. But a little to sober. Father sent me one of his, and it is a first rate picture. We are expecting to march every day so I don't know how you can write again, but do not let that hinder you from writing. When you write to father tell him I cannot write to him now, but that I am glad he sent his picture also for his well wishes. I cannot write much now but more the next time. Give my love to all the family, & my respects to all inquiring friends. You never say anything about Mrs. Simpsons folks how are they. Why don't Miss Lemain write to me. Is Charly Hinds married? From your son

W H Skinner

Camp near Gainesville June 2, 1863

Dear Mother, I have received the girls letters all of them, and the papers that have been sent, also the handkerchief and hat. I was glad to get the hat, for I was going to buy one. I hope you will continue to send me those papers. I also got Hattie's Photograph. I think it is a very good picture, but a little too faded. Father sent me one of his, and it is a first rate picture. We are expecting to march every day so I dont know how soon I can write again, but do not let that hind you from writing. When you write to Father, tell him I cannot write to him now, but that I am glad he sent his picture also for his well wishes. I cannot write much now but more the next time. Give my love to all the family, & my respects to all enquiring friends. You never say any thing about Mrs Simpsons folks how are they. Why dont Miss Jemain write to me. Is Charly Hinds married. From your Son

W. H. Skinner

Letter to Mother ... June 21st 1863

Bull Run June 21st 1863

Dear Mother I received a paper from Lucy day before yesterday but no letter. I have not had a chance to write since we left Falmouth till now, and while I am writing there is a heavy fight going on close by. I expect we will have a hand in the mess tomorrow; but maybe not. We passed over the old Bull Run battle ground yesterday. There are any quantity of hands and legs sticking out sunning themselves; besides bodies laying around half decomposed, and any number of sculls, fingers, and bones of all of the human body. Our Company have been

Bull Run June 21st 1863.

Dear Mother I received Papers from Lucy day before yesterday but no letter. I have not had a chance to write since we left Falmouth till now, and while I am writing there is a rec'd fight going on close by. I expect we will have a hand in the mess tomorrow, but maybe not — We passed over the old Bull Run battle ground yesterday. There are any quantity of hands and legs sticking out running themselves, together with skulls laying around half decomposed, and any number of skulls, fingers, and bones of the human body have been scattered. Our Company have been

Letter to Mother ... June 21st 1863

on picket to day and last night. There has been some picket firing close by and I made up my mind for a fight before night, but I guess we are all right for a good sleep tonight. I have not received any letter from Mr. Fillmore yet. Tell Mary Jane I will never forgive her if she don't write to me. I lost all those pictures the other day; Fathers, Hatties, and Marys. My knapsack bothered me so I just took my blanket out & ripped the rest to pieces, so they would be no use to any body else. But among the rest I left the pictures. Don't send any more. Can't you fix me up about a pound of chewing tobacco same as. you did the hat, with plenty of paper and send to me. Don't fail to send me those papers for I am lost if I have nothing to read. You need not send tracks, for our chaplain keeps us well supplied with them. No more at present.
Your Son
W H Skinner

Mr Pickett to day and any mine Cant you
last night. They has been fix me up about a spoon
some of Picketts flying close by of chewing tobacco same as
and I had made up my mind you did the last, with
for a fight before night, but plenty of paper and pens to
I guess we all desides that me. Don't fail to say so
in good shape to my lot of me there papers, for
have not received any letter an lost if I have nothing
from Mr Gilmore yet to read. But need not send
Will if any your girls will tracts for our chaplain and
never forgive me if I do keeps us well supplied
don't forget to ask Jurann with them. So Mrs B
I lost all those pictures brought.
the other day, Athens Yours for
etc Ain't that too G.W. Hinnis
Bringing brothers and the
lost ones Say Hostess you
add supper, the rest to
honees, if they would let
you run to any body else
But among the boys of left
the pictures, don't send

GETTYSBURG MONUMENT ... Honoring the 108th N. Y. Infantry

WORDS ON THE REVERSE SIDE OF THE GETTYSBURG MONUMENT

N. Y.
108ᵀᴴ   INFTY

OCCUPIED THIS

POSITION JULY 2 & 3, 1863

SUPPORTING BATTERY 1.1 U. S. ART.

DURING THE ARTILLERY DUEL ON THE

AFTERNOON OF JULY 3ᴿᴰ, IT

SUSTAINED A TERRIFIC FIRE

WITHOUT BEING ABLE TO RETURN A SHOT.

NUMBER ENGAGED 200.

CASUALTIES.

KILLED 16, WOUNDED 86, TOTAL 102

DURING THE CHARGE THE LEFT OF THE CONFEDERATE LINE

LAPPED ITS FRONT AND CAME WITHIN 50 YARDS

OF IT BEFORE BREAKING. THE 108ᵀᴴ N. Y. INFTY WAS

RECRUTED AND MUSTERED INTO THE SERVICE AT

ROCHESTER N. Y. AUG. 16, 1862

IT PARTICIPATED IN ALL THE BATTLES OF THE 2ᴺᴰ CORPS

FROM ANTIETAM, SEPT. 17, 1862 TO THE SURRENDER

AT APPOMATOX APR. 1865, HAVING BEEN ACTIVELY

ENGAGED   28   TIMES

Letter to Hattie ... August 1st 1863

Jarvis Hospital Aug. 1st 1863

Dear Hattie, I received a letter to day dated July 26th. The first one I have had since long before the Battle. I wish you had of sent 10 dollars instead of five for I have borrowed a good deal since the fight; as long as I have any money I might as well use some of it for if I come out safe at the end of the war I can earn more. Besides they owe us about six months pay now and I can't tell how long it will be before they will pay us. I received three papers yesterday but neither of them was the one that I spoke about, but I got a letter from the regiment and they told that there was some papers there for me and they were going to send them to me. That tobacco is there too, by the time you get this I guess I will have the whole of them. I have written to Father but had no answer yet. The war according to all appearances is pretty near an end; but we

Jarvis Hospital Aug 14th 1863

Dear Hattie, I received a letter to day dated July 26th the first one I have had since long before the Battle. I wish you had of sent 10 dollars instead of five for I have borrowed a good deal since the fight. as long as I have any money I might as well use some of it for if I come out safe at the end of the war I can earn more. Besides they owe us about six months pay now and I can't tell how long it will be before they will pay us. I received three papers yesterday but neither of them was the one I spoke about but I got a letter from the regiment and they told that there was some papers there for me and they was going to send them to me. that tobacco is there too, and by the time you get this I guess I will have the whole of them. I have written to Father but had no answer yet. The war according to all appearances is pretty near an end, but we

Letter to Hattie. . . August 1st 1863

may be deceived the same as we have been before, but I hope not, not that I have got tired of soldiering for I wish I was able to go to the regiment now and help whip out every reb and copperhead in the country north and south; I have got so I like it now and I want to have satisfaction for the 1 ½ pounds of meat that they took out of my leg. I looked around some time but I could not find it, if I had I would have slapped it in again. The shell that hit me burst just behind me and made mince meat of a horse. Direct the same as before only leave out the formerly. Don't send any more childs papers for we get plenty here. If you send any more money be sure and send greenbacks. Give my love to Mother and all the family and my respects to every body else.

From your Brother
W. H. Skinner

may be deceived the same as we have been before, but I hope not, not that I have got tired of soldiering, for I wish I was able to go to the regiment now and help whale out every reb and copperhead in the country north and south. I have got to like it now and I want to have satisfaction for the 1½ pounds of meat that they took out. My leg was looked around some time but I could not find it, if I had I would not have passed it in again. The shell that hit me burst just behind me and made mince meat of a horse. Direct the same as before only leave out the Temple. Don't send any more childs papers for we get plenty here. If you send any more money be sure and send greenbacks. Give my love to mother and all the family and my respects to every trady else.

From your Brother

W. H. Skinner

Letter to Lucy ... August 9th 1863   No original letter

Jarvis Hospital, August. 9th 1863

Dear Sister,

I received your letter yesterday; I was glad to hear you were having such fine times there. You said that Lieuts. Card(?) & Evens were killed at Vicksburg but you were mistaken. They were killed at Gettysburg and they belonged to the 108th N.Y. It is a good thing that some of the soldiers received Christian burial for there are plenty that do not. I am getting along very well but not well enough to move around much.

We have plenty to eat of the best but we have to buy the best. There is a chance for me to get a furlough now Better than it was a short time ago. I shall get well as fast as possible and get back to the regiment. I would like very much to see you all of course but there is no chance.

Tell Mother it would cost her over thirty dollars to come here and stay but about a week, and that I don't think would be a very good policy for there may be a chance yet for me to travel if no further than New York.

What do you mean by Ginger Snaps & Love? I have written to her & received no answer till I have gotten tired of it. How many dollars do you earn a day at tailoring? How do Hattie and Bill Olive get along? I would like to be there when the marriage comes off but then I could not dance so I will just sling my crutches around the room and make believe I am there. If you will tell me when it is to be.

Tell Bill to take good care of her and make a hair cushion covered with three thicknesses of trace leather for her to sit on and two iron rings in each of her ears.

Well, I will have to close now. Give my love to all the family.

From your brother   W H Skinner

Letter to Hattie ... August 12th 1863

Jarvis Hospital Aug. 12 63

Dear Sister I received your letter today. So I thought I go to work and answer it. My hands tremble so to day that I can hardly write, but I guess you can make it out with a little trouble and patience. Do not mention Mary's name to me again. I wrote a letter to Lucy yesterday. If the names of the drafted men are published in the papers, I wish you would send me one. I don't know but I will get a chance to come home a while when I can get around. There is no use to send anything here for I can get every thing I want cheaper than they could be sent from there. If I should not get home you must not be disappointed for my place is with my regiment, and I have always been satisfied there, and ever since I have been wounded and away from it, I have been lonesome. Give my love to all the family. from your brother.

W H Skinner

Armory Square Hospital Aug 12/63

Dear friend Sherlock I received your letter to day. I go through it and I would go to morrow and answer it. Now hopes from me to say that I am hardly able to sit up to write. But I guess I can (maybe) it only with a little exercise and patience. May I do not mention my name by me again. Please write a letter to say yesterday to Gil that they named the drafted men are published the papers, I don't know if you would get one. I am not get

a chance to come home a while when there is can get around. There is no use to send any thing here to I can get many thing that they could be sent from there If I should not get them you must not be disappointed for my place is with my regiment and have always been satisfied there, and ever since I have been wounded and was brought I have been lonesome. Give my love to all the family from your Brother W H Thunner

Letter to Mother ... August 1863

Aug- 63

Dear Mother
*   I have written two letters to and I have received no answer don't know what is the reason and I gave you the directions to write to me. Direct to Camp Palmer Company F. 108th Regt. N.Y.V. Washington D.C. I have been well ever since I left for I have taken care of myself.. Tell the girls to write whether I do or not, and I will write as often as I can. Tell Mary Jane to write too. I promised to write to her but I can't do it all at once. J says he dreamed last night that Hattie was dead and he was to the funeral. Buy Dewitt a pound of candy for me. Tell George to learn to play the fiddle by the time I get back. Give my respects to every body. and don't forget Mary, tell me who she has got for a Beau now and don't let her know it.*
*   Write right away*

*   Your son*
*   W H Skinner*

aug - 63

Dear Mother
 I have written two letters to and I have received no answer I dont know what is the reason and I gave you the directions to write to me Direct to Camp Palmer Company F, 108th Regt N.Y.V. Washington D.C. I have been well ever since I left for I have taken care of myself tell the girls to write whether I do or not, and I will write as often as I can tell Mary Jane to write too I promised to write to her but I cant do it all at once I say he dreamed last night that Hatty was dead and he was to the funeral, buy Dewitt a pound of candy for me Tell George to learn how to play the fiddle by the time I get back Give my respects to every body and don't forget Mary, tell me who she has got for a Beaux now and don't let her know it.
 write right away

 Your Son
 W.H. Rinine

Letter to Lucy ... September 8th 1863   No original letter

Jarvis Hospital Sept. 8th 1863

Dear Sister I received your letter of the 28th August with seven dollars. I suppose you are all well as you do not say any different. I am getting along finely now. I have thrown my crutches one side and walk with a cane. It is pretty hard work but it is better than carrying a pair of crutches around.

I have something else to tell you. Sunday morning I had just woke up from a nap when Father came walking in. It took me rather by surprised for I did not expect him. He had no trouble finding me. He will sleep in the same room while he remains here and eat at the government table if he wishes. There is a man from Rochester has been here with his brother in law nearly two months.

I will get six months pay in a few days. Do not send any more money.

If I am not mistaken I will get well enough to go to the regiment in a month or six weeks. Tell Mother not to worry about me at all for I am doing as well as possible. Is Bill Olmsted home again? I wonder what is the reason. Benjamin Allen has not answered my letters. Father is going to stay ten or twelve days here.. He is very much pleased with the place. How is DeWitt & Martha & George?

Sunday afternoon Father and myself & another young man took a walk. We went through by one of the forts the "Darks" have built around this city.

It is now dinner time. I will close. Give my love to Mother and all the family.

W H Skinner

Letter to Sister ... September 28th 1863

Jarvis Hospital Sept. 28, 63

Dear Sister. I am getting along so well that I thought I would get a picture for you. You will see by that that I have not failed much in flesh since I left home. Since I have succeeded in burning the gangrene out of my wound, it has been healing rapidly but I will not have the use of my leg for a some time after it is healed I expect Father is home by this time, as he said he would leave New York in a week after he left here. There is no sign of our being sent away from here yet. I have nothing much to write about at present. Give my love to Mother & all the rest.

W H Skinner

Lincoln Hospital Sept. 28, 63.

Dear Sister

I am getting
along nicely. Is you get well
by the time I get well that
— I would get a picture for
you. You will see by that
that I have not failed
ever since I left home
since I have succeeded in burning
the fingers out of my
wound. It had been
healing to previous but
would not have Closed
in my leg for some
time after it is neglected
I expect. Father is home
by this time as he said
he would leave Newport
in a week after he left
here. There is no dyer of
our being sent away

from here yet. I
have not hing much
to write about at
present. Give my
love to the rest

W. H. Skinner

Brother - George Washington Lafayette Skinner

b. 4 September 1850 in N.Y. City

d. 12 December 1920 in Rochester, N.Y.

Picture about 1916

Brother - DeWitt Clinton Skinner

b. 13 August 1859 in Rochester, N.Y.

d. 13 April 1949 in Rochester, N.Y.

Picture about 1911

Left card

S. | 108 | N.Y.

William Skinner

S..., Co. F, 108 Reg't N. Y. Infantry.

Appears on

Company Muster Roll

for Sept & Oct, 1863.

Present or absent: Absent

Stoppage, $ 100 for ....

Due Gov't, $ 100 for ....

Remarks: Wounded at the battle of Gettysburg, Pa July 3/63

Book mark: ....

(358)   Copyist

Right card

S. | 108 | N.Y.

W. C. Skinner

Oct, Co. F, 108 Reg't N.Y.

Appears on

Hospital Muster Roll

of Jarvis U. S. A. General Hospital,

at Baltimore, Md.,

for Sept & Oct, 1863.

Attached to hospital:

When ...., 186 .

How employed ....

Last paid by Maj ....

to ...., 186 .

Bounty paid $ 100; due $ 100

Present or absent ....

Remarks: On furlough since Oct, 17.

Book mark: ....

Sister – Harriet (Hattie) Elizabeth Skinner

b.   *7 December 1843 in N. Y. City*

d.   *1 February 1918 in Rochester N. Y.*

Picture about 1863

Sister – Lucy Ann Skinner

b.   *5 December 1845 in N Y City*

m-1   *1868 to Francis Penny in Rochester, NY*

m-2   *14 January 1923 to Wealthy Rogers in Kenmore, NY*

d.   *3 April 1931 in Kenmore, NY*

No picture available

Letter to Hattie ... November 19th 1863

Jarvis U. S. A. General Hospital
Baltimore, Md.   November 19, 1863

Dear Sister,

Here I am again back to my old home in Baltimore; it seems just as natural as ever; left New York Monday night at half past eleven o'clock and arrived here at six Tuesday morning. Tried to get transferred to N. Y. but met with no success. Left Jim Bowman at Central Park Hospital. The folks are all glad to see me come back again. The weather is much warmer and pleasanter here than it was there. Tell Father that on account of my short

Jarvis U. S. A. General Hospital,

Baltimore, Md. November 19, 1863.

Dear Sister,

Here I am again back to my old home in Baltimore, it seems just as natural as ever. Left New York Monday night at half past eleven o'clock and arrived here at six Tuesday morning. Tried to get transferred to N.Y. but met with no success. Left Jim Bowman at Central Park Hospital. The folks were all glad to see me come back again. The weather is much warmer and pleasanter here than it was there. Tell Father that, on account of my short

Letter to Hattie ... November 19th 1863

stay in New York I had no chance to get a coat and besides it was raining hard while I was there and when we left so I had to wear it for fear of catching cold; am very sorry it happened so; tell him to take the price of it out of the bank. Please send those letters to me that have been sent there; as soon as I got here the boys purchased a violin for me and some other instruments; we are going to form a string band and amuse ourselves as long as we remain here. I went to see Aunt Ann and Lizzy while I was in N. Y. They were very glad to see me. Tell Father I saw Mr. Sherman. He will tend to those thing;. I staid in Central Park Hospital Sunday night with Jim; did not like it so well as I do here; suppose Lucy sent that note I gave her. Tell John to dig in for I am done picking up potatoes & husking corn for awhile; my best respects to Fanny Faker. My love to Mother and all the rest.

From your brother
W H Skinner

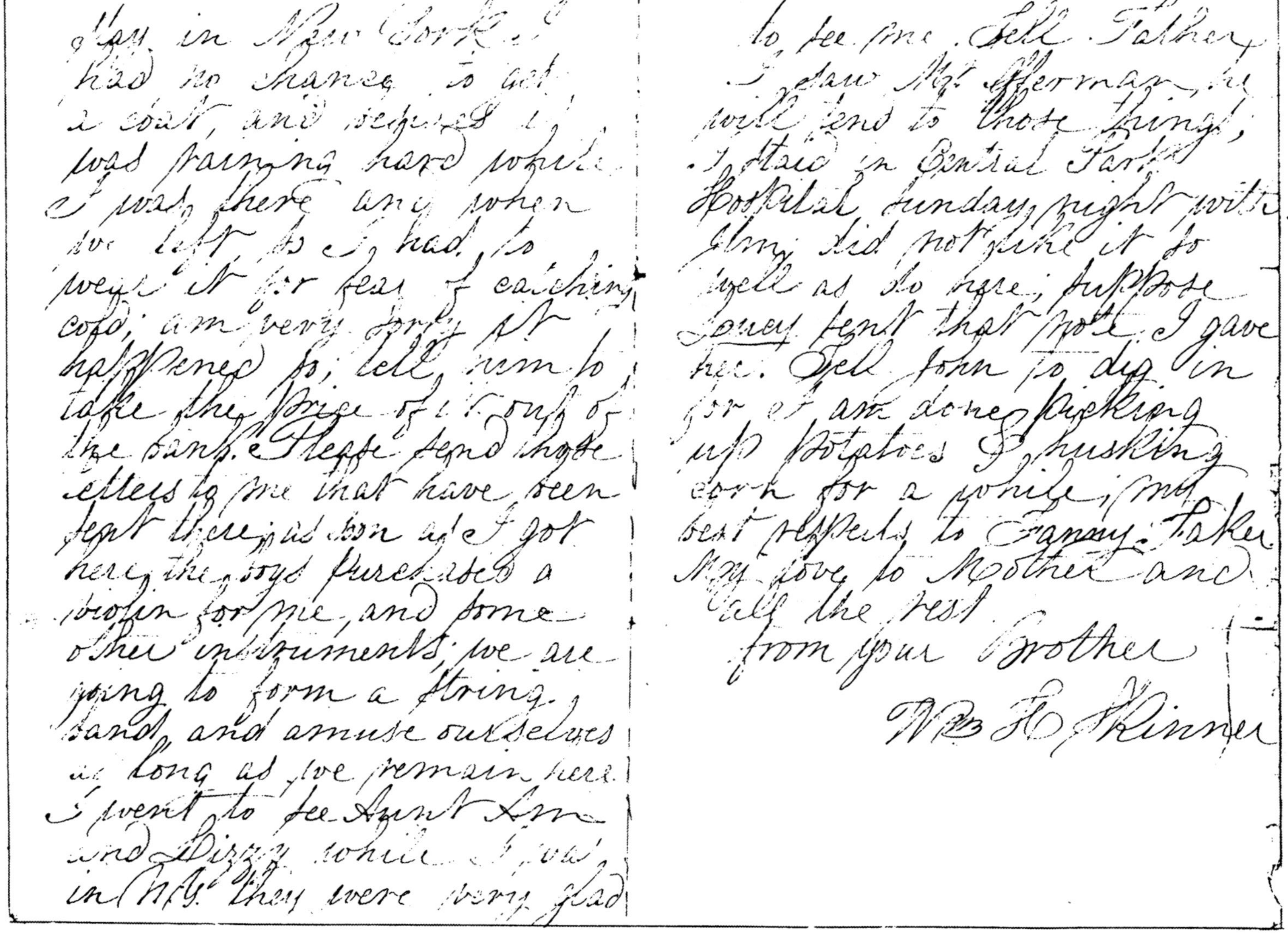

[Handwritten letter, largely illegible cursive. Partial transcription:]

...up in high spirits... had no chance to eat... I could find any respite... had nothing hard to... I was there very sorry... but I left for few...

...to see me, tell Father... I gave my afternoon... would send to there things... I stay in boarding houses... I stayed sunday night until... Army had not gained its... well as so far, suppose... they kept there post, I gave... free. Tell him to try... for I am done hauling... up potatoes & husking... corn for a young man... best properly to company Parker... may move to mother and... all the rest...

from your brother
Wm H Stringer

Letter to Lucy ... November 22nd 1863   No original letter

Jarvis Hospital Nov. 22nd 1863

Dear Sister

I wrote to Hattie a day or two ago and as I have nothing to do just now I shall write to you. It is Sunday morning and as beautiful a day as you would wish to see. Besides we have just eaten a splendid breakfast sent to us by two young " Ladies" across the street. You probably heard me speak of them while at home.

We had a good time here in our room last night. We had two violins, two banjoes, a bass viola and a flute. Besides some good singers. Also some young ladies who came in to see us so you see we are not going to die of ennui.

The doctors have christened us the happy family and call our rooms the temple of mirth.

Please tell Father that Messrs Scott & Farriand who were wounded in the feet, are doing well.

I shall not receive any pay for two months on account of not being present at muster. I wish you would ask mother to find me one ten dollar greenback and I will replace it when I get my pay.

The boys all join in sending their respects to Father.

I would be very glad to have you send one of your photographs; also one of Hattie's. I wish you would send me my black neck-tie in a paper. I have not found any here like it. Oh this is a splendid morning. The sun is shinning so warm.

Well Lucy, I hardly know what to fill up with so I guess I will draw This to a close. and go to church.

Give my love to Mother and all the family.

From your Brother
W H Skinner

Letter to Father … December 11th 1863   **No original letter**

JARVIS W. S. General Hospital
Baltimore Dec. 11, 1863

Dear Father,

Your paper & letters were received last evening. The paper was quite a treat being the first Rochester print I have had the pleasure of reading in the hospital. My wound is not healed up yet. It is very sore. I do not know but they will probably keep me till spring.

The doctors are very anxious to have me join the string band. I don't know but I shall if my wound doesn't get better. We also have a brass band practicing every day and progressing finally.

I had a letter from Jim yesterday. He is now in Alexandria Va. In the convalescent camp. He will probably be transferred to the invalid core.

The weather here is splendid. No rain since I've been back. The draft went off very quietly here. No disturbance of any kind.

We anticipate having a pretty good time on Christmas as we (room N) have received invitations down town. Enclosed are some verses composed by Charles Fauand who it seems, understood that I was married.

I would like very much to have any papers sent here that contain any news of the 108th Reg. as I have not heard from the boys in some time.

While in New York I became acquainted with several of your friends. They were glad to see me. All inquired about you. Aunt Ann thought I rather beat you getting home before you.

Not having anything more of interest to write about. I will close by sending my love to mother & all the family.

                              From your Son
                              W. H. Skinner

Letter to Sister ... January 15th 1864

Jarvis Hospital   Jan. 15 64

Dear Sister

Yours of the 11th was received this morning. Was pleased to know that you are all enjoying good health. I have been well enough with the exception of my wound, which is not healed yet but is very painful. There was an examination of the convalescents here day before yesterday. There was about 40 who were sent to their Regiments; some of them to my company. But I could not go; shall try and go next time there are any sent. Don't know what you mean by two or three coming down here, unless you mean those two pictures; but I was not surprised to see them because I sent for them; but as you do not seem to want me to have them, I sent them back as you requested. It is all bosh about my being a Seargent; have just had a letter from the Regt. and from that it is not so; am just as well satisfied.
My love to all.

W. H. S.

Give the note enclosed to Mother

Jarvis Hospital Jan 15th

Dear Sister

Yours of the 11th was received this morning was pleased to know that you are all enjoying good health. I have sufficient enough with the exception of my wound, which is not healed yet, but is nearly well. There was an examination of the conscripts here day before yesterday, there was about 40 who were sent to their Regiments. Some of them to my company. But I could not go, shall try and go next time there are any sent. Dont know what you mean by two or three coming down here, unless you mean those two pictures, but I was not disposed to let them because I sent for them, just as you do not seem to want time to have them, I say them away as you requested. All is well about my being in Sergeants, have just had a letter from the Regt. has found that it is not so. Am just as well satisfied. My love to all.

W.O.S

Give the note enclosed, to Mother

| | 108 | N.Y. |

Wm Skinner

Pvt., Co. F, 108 Reg't N. Y. Infantry.

Appears on

Company Muster Roll

for Jan & Feb, 1864.

Present or absent Absent

Stoppage, $ 100 for

Due Gov't, $ 100 for

Remarks: Wounded at Gettysburg July 3rd /63

Book mark:

| S | 108 | N.Y. |

W. H. Skinner

Pvt., Co. F, 108 Reg't N.Y.

Appears on

Hospital Muster Roll

of Jarvis U. S. A. General Hospital,

at Baltimore, Md.,

for Jan & Feb, 1864.

Attached to hospital:

When ...., 186 .

How employed ....

Last paid by Maj. ....

to ...., 186 .

Bounty paid $ 100; due $ 100

Present or absent Absent

Remarks: On furlough since Feb. 17/64

Book mark:

No. 2111 Requisition for Transportation of U. S. Troops,
Issued **March 2ed 1864**
On Agent ....Erie Railway .... R. R.
at ....Rochester .... for Transportation
of ....Wm. H...Skinner Co....F....................
........108th....N Y...V...
From......Rochester....To.............Baltimore................
Via..................................Furlough..................
............212241.....................................
By ....

Letter to Mother ... March 25th 1864

Jarvis Hospital   March 25   64

Dear Mother.

Your kind letter was received yesterday; had begun think nobody was going to write to me. It is now a little after eleven o'clock. It is rather late in the evening to be writing, but I must be doing something to keep me awake. But I suppose you are wondering what keeps me up so late, so I will tell you. When we were reassigned, they wanted me to go to the invalid Corps. But I told them that I wanted to go to my regiment instead; but they did not see fit to send me, so they placed me in charge of the house; and I am now acting in the capacity of nurse; have got to see that everything about the house is as it should be; in other words I am commander in chief of the several disabled men in the brick house. So you see I am fixed for another period of two months. We have some very bad cases; we have to sit up all night with them; but we take turns at it, so it is not hard work.

The folks at the landing called Jim a hospital "beat" Christian me the same; but every "beat" can't show so large a scare.

I am very thankful for what you sent me and as soon as we are paid I shall send

Jarvis Hospital Mar 23 '64

Dear Mother

Your kind letter was received yesterday, had begun to think nobody was going to write to me. It is now a little after eleven o'clock P.M. rather late in the evening to be writing, and I must be doing something to keep me awake. But you know you are wondering what keeps me up so late, so I will tell you. When we were rearranged they wanted me to go in the ward but — I told them that I only — I told them that I wanted to go to my Regiment indeed, but they did insist to fit to send me, so they placed me in charge of the House, and I am now acting in the capacity

of steward, have got to see that everything about the house is as it should be, in other words I am Commander in Chief of the several detailed men in the brick house. So you see I am fixed for another period of two months. We have some very bad cases, we have to set up all night with them, but we take turns at it, so it is but hard duty. The officer at the Landing called for a hospital beat off, and I presume they will consider me the patient, they may beat I can't stay so large a bear.

I am very thankful for what you sent me and as soon as we are paid shall send

73

Letter to Mother … March 25th 1864

to you with the rest. I am glad that ring pleases Father so much, but I guess he will have to handle a good many cords of wood to hurt it much. That party you spoke of I suppose was a marry one, and I would like to have been there, but I have saved ten cents by being absent. If you should happen to hear of my being married, do not be surprised, I did know of a girl in York State that would have suited me better, but there is no accounting for the curious notions that some of them have. You are good at guessing; but I shall guess a little; so I guess I shall stop writing any more on that subject. I have not heard from New York since I've been back hear. Give my respect to Hall's folks and every body else that cares for them.

> *From your*
> *affectionate son*
> *W H Skinner*

Please write soon

To you I write this not. I am
addition my pen, please Father
by any middle guess he will
have to handle a good many
cords of wood to hurt it. If M.
Chad Thorpe spoke I sup-
-pose was had a merry time and
I would indeed to have any
but I have saved ten cents by
being absent. If you should
happen to hear of my being mar-
-ried do not be surprised. I do
know of a good in York state
that would be suited me better
but there is no acounting for
the curious notions that some
of them have. You are good at
guessing, guess I shall quess a
little, so I guess I shall stop
writing any more on that sub-
-ject. I write not heard from

New York since I've
been back here. Give my
best respects to
Father & folly
tell them I [...] by & see that
cannot for them.
From your
Affectionate [...]
W. Mm[...]

Letter to Mother ... April 1st 1864

Jarvis Hospital   Apr. 1/64

Dear Mother.

We have just been paid and now send you the five dollars that you were kind enough to give me. Why don't you write to me oftener than once a month. There are but one or two others that I shall write to now and I shall drop them if they do not write oftener than you have. Here it is nearly a month since I've been back here and only three letters; and but one from home.

If I join the navy as I have been contemplating lately, there will not be as good a chance to get letters as now; so you had better make the most of the time which will be short.

There, one of the lady nurses has just succeeded in fooling me.

I have written to Mr. Fillmore but a short time since; have received no answer. I do not have so much time to run around now as I used to have since I've been nursing. Still I manage to enjoy myself pretty well. No more at present. My love to all the family.

From your son
W H Skinner

Army Hospital April 16

Dear Father

I have just been paid, and now send you the ___ dollars that you was kind enough to give me. Why don't you write me oftener than once a month? There are but one or two others.

I shall write to you and ___ drop them if they do not ___ oftener than you have. Once it is nearly a month since I ___ been back ___ and only three letters, and one from home.

If I join the navy as I have been contemplating lately, there will not be so good chance to get letters as now, so you had better make the most of the time. ___ will be short.

There, one of the lady nurses any just succeeded in shooting me, and I have written to Mr Fillmore but a short time since, have received no answer. I do not have so much time to run around now as I used to have since I've been nursing still. I manage to enjoy myself pretty well. My love to all the ___ family. From your son

W. L. Gamms

Letter to Sister ... April 11th 1864

Jarvis Hospital April 11, 64

Dear Sister,

Yours of the 7th was received about twenty minutes ago and as I have nothing to do just at present, I thought it would be a good time to answer it. Henry Jones came to see me today; tried to have him stay and have dinner with me but he said he had just laid in a stock of oysters; and could not eat any dinner.

I presume you have heard of the death of Frank Simpson before this time. I saw him once when he was sick and had no reason to believe that he would not get well; but the boys say that he was home sick, and complained of being home sick; I have known more than a dozen

Jarvis Hospital, April 11, 64.

Dear Sister,

Yours of the 7th was received about twenty minutes ago, and as I have nothing to do just at present, I thought it would be a good time to answer it. Henry Jones came up to see me to day, tried to have him stay and have dinner with me, but he said he had just laid in a stock of oysters, and could not eat any dinner.

I presume you have heard of the death of Frank Simpson before this time. Saw him once when he was sick, and had no reason to believe that he would not get well, but the boys say that he was home-sick, and complained of being "......". I have known more than a dozen

Letter to Sister ... April 11th 1864

in our regiment to die from that very same cause, and that, I think, was the cause of his death. We expect every day some men to fill up the hospital; there are seven hundred of released prisoners from Richmond coming here and I shall have my ward filled up.

They are most all sick or wounded. I don't see what makes you think I am counting the weeks and days already, for I have not given it a thought yet. That twenty five dollars a month would be very nice, no doubt; but if I ever get it until I work by the month on a farm. I shall never have the pleasure of earning that amount; if I had a farm of my own that would be a different thing; then I should take pleasure in working it. But you need not be alarmed about my joining the navy for they would not accept me on account of my wound. but I confess that I wish they had for I want to try a change of program. Why don't you send me some papers once in a while as you used to do or do you think I have not time to read them I sent a paper to George a few days ago; tell him to write me a letter in return; tell him to keep those tooth picks for they were made of wishbone of a cow. No more at present. My love to all. From

Your Brother,
William

P.S. If you see George Lutes, tell him I am waiting for an answer to that letter.

in our Regiment to die from
that very fancy cause, and that
I think, was the cause of his death.
We expect every day some men to fill
up the hospital, there are seven
hundred of wheated prisoners from
Richmond coming here, and I
shall have my ward filled up.
They are most all sick or
wounded. I dont see what use you
think I am counting the
weeks and days already for I
have not given it a thought yet.
That twenty five dollars a month
would be very nice, no doubt, but
it never yet, until lately, did
the month on a farm, my bill
never has the expense of running
the amount. If I had a farm
of my own it would be a different
thing, then I should take pleasure
in working it. But you need be

ashamed about my joining the
navy, for they would not accept
me on account of my wound.
But I confess that I with they
had, for I wanted to try a change
of programme. My wound is present
the same looking piece in a future
as you used to do, or do you think
I have not time to of act things.
I sent a paper to George a few
days ago, tell him to expect me a
letter in return, tell him to keep
those tools — pick for when you
made of the wood — hay of ye cow
the pine — and pretend. My love to
all. Jim
Your Brother
William

P.S. If you see George Lutes, tell
him I am waiting for an
answer to that letter

Letter to George ... April 20th 1864

Jarvis Hospital   April 20th 1864

Dear Brother

I received your letter this morning; was pleased to see that you could write such a good long letter and I must say that you give me more of the particulars than the rest do; but you must be more particular the next time you write, and not get your words mixed together so much; and get your spelling more correct; though your spelling now is as good as Hatties. There were two toothpicks in that paper; one in the shape of a foot, and the other was a long square one.

Have you learned to play any tunes on the fiddle yet? I wish you were here with me; I have a fiddle in my room all the time; if you was here I could soon learn you to play. That is a first rate picture of you George; you was at school when I left that day so I could not say good bye. But never mind I will have a chance again some day or other if everything happens and nothing goes right.

I wrote a letter to Hattie this morning and received one from Jim Bowman; he is going to the Regiment pretty soon. I hope your geese will hatch all their eggs. Will Bennatter was very foolish not to play with you that night, if it had been me I should tell Mother. I received the letter with the fifty cents. The wishbone of a cow lays close under the tail. I am glad that pudding is so good; wish I had some. We have pudding for dinner nearly every day.

Jarvis Hospital April 20th 1864

Dear Brother

I received your letter this morning, was pleased to see that you could write such a good long letter, and I must say that you give me more of the particulars than the rest do: but you must be more particular the next time you write, and not get your words mixed together so much, and get your spelling more correct; though your spelling now is as good as Hattie's. There were two tooth picks in that paper, one in the shape of a foot, and the other was a long square one.

Have you learned to play any tunes on the fiddle yet? I wish you was here with me; I have a fiddle in my room all the time; if you was here I could soon learn you to play; That is a firstrate picture of you George; you was at school when I left that day, so I could not say good bye. But never mind I will have a chance again some day or other if everything happens and nothing goes right.

I wrote a letter to Hattie this morning, and received one from Jim Bowman; he is going to the Regiment pretty soon. I hope your geese will hatch all their eggs. Will Bennatter was very foolish not to stay with you that night, if it had of been me I should. Tell Mother I received the letter with the fifty cents. The with bone of a cow lays close under the tail. I am glad that pudding is so good, wish I had some. We have pudding for dinner nearly every day.

83

Letter to George ... April 20th 1864

Well George I did have a belly full; but it was because you had the words mixed up so much. When you write again don't be afraid to write a good long letter and tell me everything that is going on, as you did in this one; and if that is your first attempt at writing I think you have done very well. You had better hurry and get washed and eat your dinner. Yes I know the meadow behind the house so you are going to have a orchard there are you. I shall not laugh at your writing, so you can go & eat your dinner. Tell George Lutes I have written him two letters and had only one from him; the last one I sent, I asked him to send me three or four pounds of tobacco by express, and I would send him the Greenbacks; when you see him tell him to send it. Who plays on the other piano. You had better hurry and find that shoe of Bill's. Well I shall quit now. Write soon again. Give my love to all.

From your brother
W H Skinner

Well George I did have a billy fall; but it was because you had the words mixed up so much. When you write again don't be afraid to write a good long letter and tell me every thing that is going on, as you did in this one; and if that is your first attempt at writing I think you have done very well. You had better hurry and get washed and eat your dinner. Yes I know the meadow behind the house; So you are going to have an orchard there are you. I shall not laugh at your writing, so you can go and eat your dinner. Tell George Writes I have written him two letters and only had one from him; the last one I sent, I asked him to send me three or four pounds of tobacco by express, and I would send him the Greenbacks; when you see him tell him to send it. Who plays on the other piano. You had better hurry and find that shoe of Bill's. Well I shall quit now. Write soon again. Give my love to all.

From Your Brother W. H. Skinner.

Letter to Hattie ... April 28th 1864

Jarvis Hospital   April 28th 1864

Dear Sister,

    Your letter was received today, and as I have nothing in particular to do I thought I would pass away part of the time writing another. You want to know who my cousin is and what his name is; well it don't happen to be a he, but a she; and her name is Maggie Moore. I was to a party one evening, where there were six cousins, all young ladies; so I asked if I could not find a cousin and Maggie said she would be my cousin and so she is pretty. I agreed and we are known as cousins. Those lines did not apply to Evelyn. Those prisoners I spoke of, I did not mention as belonging to my Regiment. I sent a letter to John Olfex in care of George; give it to him as soon as you see him. Tell Lucy that I cannot write to all so my letters must answer for the whole family. Tell Martha it took me only twenty five minutes to read her letter. Will send you my wife's picture some of these days.

    I have not had a letter from Lizzie Blanchard since I've been here. No more at present. My love to all.

From your Brother
W H Skinner

Jarvis Hospital. April 28th 1864.

Dear Sister.

Your letter was received to-day, and as I have nothing in particular to do I thought I would pass away part of my time writing another. You want to know who my Cousin is and what his name is; well it dont happen to be a he, but a she; and her name is Maggie Moore. I was to a party one evening where there were six cousins, all young ladies; so I asked if I could not find a cousin, and Maggie said she would be my cousin; and as she is pretty I agreed, and we are known as cousins. Those lines did not apply to Evelyn. Those prisoners I spoke of, I did not mention as belonging to my Regiment. I sent a letter to John Green in care of George; give it to him as soon as you see him. Tell Lucy that I cannot write to all, so my letters must answer for the whole family. Tell Martha it took me only twenty five minutes to read her letter. Will send you my Wife's Picture some of these days.

I have not had a letter from Lizzie Blanchard since I've been here. No more at present. My love to all. From your Brother

W. H. Skinner.

Letter to Hattie ... May 8th 1864

Jarvis Hospital
Baltimore Md.
May 8th 1864

Dear Sister.

Here it is Sunday again; time about two o'clock and I writing another letter. Write often enough I reckon, don't I? How is the state of of the weather up their? Right about yue, as some of the Baltimoreans say, it is gloriously hot; but the evenings are delightful. I sometimes sit out on the porch with my brier root, sometimes take a walk in Union Square with my cousin. I must finish this by half past two for the bugler will blow the church call, and I must be ready. I go every Sunday. Our Chapel is not very large; will not hold more than two hundred and fifty persons; it is most always filled though; and one quarter of them are ladies. No pay for me this time; took it for transportation; owe them about eight dollars still, which will be taken out next Sunday. So you see that for the pleasure of spending a few days at home, I have got to be without any money two months longer. Interesting, is it not? No use though of crying over spilled milk.

Lewis Hospital.
Atlanta Rd.
August 5th 1864.

Dear Sister.

It is Sunday
again, sometime about two o'clock,
and I write another letter,
write often enough I reckon;
don't I? How is the state of
the weather up there? I thought
about you, as some of the Battle-
men say, it is gloriously hot.
But the evenings are delightful.
Sometimes I get out on the
porch with my friend Post, sometimes take a walk on Tiney Baynes
with my Cousin. I must finish

this by half past two, for the
bugle will blow the church call
and I must be ready to go every
Sunday. Our Chapel is not very
large, will not hold more than
two hundred and fifty persons; it
is not always filled though, and
about one quarter of them are
ladies. Pay day for me this time.
took it for twenty-two or
them about eight dollars still,
which will be taken out next
pay day. So you see that for the
pleasure of spending a few days
at home I have got to go without
any money two months longer.
Interesting, is it not? to lose
though of crying over spilled milk.

Letter to Hattie ... May 8th 1864

By all accounts, I presume they are having glorious sport down in Virginia. Our core, and of course our Regiment, have had a share of it. Oh I wish I was there, for this summer will end it, and I do want to see it out; but they wont let the nurses go for they expect to have plenty of wounded men here, as they have orders to prepare for eight hundred more. We have now about 500 men; they are building wards every day. I wish I could have my room filled up with boys from my Regt. I have not much to do now for I have but two patients in the whole house and they are able to help themselves. Don't forget those photographs. I have sent you two letters that I have not heard from. Tell George not to forget his letters. No more at present. My love to mother and all the rest.

From your Brother
Wm. H Skinner

By all accounts, I presume, they are having glorious sport down in Virginia. Our Com- and of course our Reg'ment have had a share of it. Oh I wish I was there for this summer will end it, and I do want to see it out; but they won't let the nurses go, for they expect to have plenty if we send men boys as they have ordered to prepare for eight hundred more. We have now about 500 men; they are buying wards every day. I wish I could have you from Toledo up with boys from my Reg't. I have not much to do now. So I hang but two patients in the whole house and they are able

to help themselves. I forgot those Photographs. I have sent you two letters that I have not heard from. Tell George not to forget his letter. No more at present. My love to Mother and all the rest.

From your Brother,
Wm H Skinner.

Walter

Letter to George ... May 12th 1864

Jarvis U. S. A. Gen'l Hospital
Baltimore, Md. May 12th 1864

Well George, I have just reached the starting point toward writing you a good long letter; for you write the longest letters that I receive, and I will try & do the same for you this time. Don't know that I shall be able to find news enough to fill this sheet, but if I can't today, will finish tomorrow, or some day between this and the fourth of July. The weather has been very hot for about a week, but today it is cloudy and cool. Here comes a couple of the boys to play Whist. There they are filling their pipes and preparing for their game; Their names are Walter Dunn, and Sam Fulmer. Sam asked me to take a hand but I excused myself and told him to wait until Christmas. Since that soldier kicked the bucket yesterday morning, one of my old patients has been sent back to me. I was busy yesterday nearly all day; had to prepare the house for wounded men; put up several beds and get everything in order; that job is done and I have nothing to do but amuse myself until the men arrive. Well George, I will have to light my pipe now; guess I can smoke and write at once. George, just wait a few minutes till I go to the office and get some passes for the boys; that is done, now I will proceed. There I must stop again; one of the boys has stumped me to pitch a game of quoits. The game with several more is finished, and my partner and I are the bullies. We have plenty of sport pitching quoits and playing ball. Do you ever pitch? How do you get along with the fiddle?

Jarvis U.S.A. Gen'l Hospital.
Baltimore Md. May 12th 1864.

Well George, I have just reached the starting point towards writing you a good long letter; for you write me the longest letters that I receive, and I will try & do the same for you this time. Don't know that I shall be able to find news enough to fill this sheet, but if I can't to day, will finish tomorrow, or some day between this and the fourth of July. The weather has been very hot for about a week, but to day it is cloudy and cool. Here comes a couple of the Boys to day. "Hist." There, they are filling their pipes and preparing for their game; their names are Wally Dunn, and Sam Turner. Sam asked me to take a hand, but I excused myself and told 'm to wait till Christmas. Since that soldier kicked the bucket yesterday morning, one of my old patients has been sent back to me. I was busy yesterday nearly all day; had to prepare the house for wounded men; put up several beds and get everything in order; that job is done and I have nothing to do but amuse myself untill the men arrive. Well George, I will have to light my pipe now; guess I can smoke and write at once. George, just wait a few minutes till I go to the office and get some passes for the boys; that is done, now I will proceed. There, I must stop again, one of the boys has stumped me to pitch a game of quoits. The game, with several more is finished, and my partner and I are the bullies. We have plenty of sport pitching quoits and playing ball. Do you ever pitch? How do you get along with the fiddle?

93

Letter to George ... May 12th 1864

I have just been to dinner, and I feel so good, so I will write a little more. Since I commenced this letter I have stopped four or five times already; don't know how long it will be before I will finish it but will endeavor to have it done by Saturday.

It is raining now, but it don't bother me any for I don't have to go out in it. Why don't the girls send me some papers once in a while as they used to? George you must try and spell a little better than you do, although you are improving; and you must make a capital I every time you speak of yourself; For instance, if you write, I am going to school. And every time you write the name of a place, or the name of a person, use a capital to begin with. There is an old wench burning coffee out in the kitchen where Father eat dinner one day. She burns coffee here every day. We had a dinner of beef, cabbage, bread, & pudding to day. You did not tell me in your last letter of anyone getting married; they are not going to stop the fun already are they? One of those girls across the way is looking for some music for me; she has about a two horse wagon box full of it, and she is overhauling it to find what I want. Here it is Thursday, afternoon, one o'clock, and I have not received that tobacco that George Lutes said he was going to send last Thursday; it should have been here last Monday. If you see him ask him if he directed it the same as he did the letter, and whether it was in a box or a package. The bugler sleeps in my house up stairs, and he wakes me up every morning and evening and inspection of the wards every Sunday. It has stopped raining and the sun is trying to shine again, it is nice and cool now; cool enough to have a game of baseball. There is a large drove of Uncle Sam's cattle just going past.

I have just been to dinner, and I feel so better as good, so I will write a little more. Since I commenced this letter I have stopped four or five times allready; don't know how long it will be before I will finish it, but will endeavor to have it done by Saturday. It is raining now, but it don't bother me any, for I don't have to go out in it. Why don't the girls send me some papers once in a while as they used to. George, you must try and spell a little better than you do, although you are improving; and you must make a capital I every time you speak of yourself, for instance if you write, I am going to school. And every time you write the name of a place, or the name of a person, use a capital to begin with. There is an old person burning coffee out in the kitchen where Father eat dinner one day. She burns coffee here every day. We had a dinner of beef, cabbage, bread & pudding to day. You did not tell me in your last letter of any one getting married, they are not going to stop the fun allready are they? One of those girls across the way is looking for some music for me, she has about a two horse wagon box full of it, and she is overhauling it to find what I want. Here it is Thursday, afternoon, one oclock, and I have not received that tobacco that George Loutes said he was going to send last Thursday; it should of been here last monday. If you see him ask him if he directed it the same as he did the letter, and whether it was in a box or a package. The bugler sleeps in my house up stairs, and he wakes me up every morning at six oclock for roll call. We have roll call every morning and evening, and inspection of the wards every Sunday. It had stopped raining and the sun is trying to shine again, it is nice and cool now; cool enough to have a game of base ball. There is a large drove of Uncle Sam's cattle just going past.

Letter to George ... May 12th 1864

We don't have any chickens to eat here, as you was telling about, but we have plenty of everything that Uncle Sam allows. I guess the sun will not succeed in getting out again to day, for a heavy cloud has just covered it again. Have you got all your potatoes and corn planted yet? I will give you your board for your clothes, if you throw all those stones down the bank; you can get plenty of jobs, and make lots of money, so I would advise you to go to work as soon as possible. Sam is oiling his stump now; he has got a wooden leg, but he can not wear it long at a time yet. The company of invalids on guard at this hospital are going to be paid to day. Well George, I guess I will lay this by till tomorrow for I can't think of anything more just now; besides, there will probably be something turning up by tomorrow night; so good bye until then. Friday morning May 13/64 Good morning, George, Since writing the above, I have received the tobacco; it was brought to me yesterday afternoon so you need not see George Lutes about it. I am going down town to get a violin string in a few minutes. We had one of our concerts last night; we had a fiddle, banjo, guitar, and base viol; had our concert where we always do on the porch. The government wagons are just going down town to work; there are about 100 of them; they go down every morning, and come back every evening. I have not seen the Jones's boys in about a week; guess I will go and see them today. Here comes our wench again to burn coffee. I wrote to Jim Bowman about two weeks ago; have not heard from him yet. George, I will give you a description of my room; see how you like it. It is about two thirds as large as your school room, and has three large windows, two of them open on the porch.

We don't have any chickens to eat here, as you was telling about, but we have plenty of every thing that Uncle Sam allows. I guess the sun will not succeed in getting out again to day, for a heavy cloud has just hidded it again. Have you got all your potatoes and corn planted yet? I will give you your board for your clothes, if you will throw all of those stories down the bank, you can get plenty of jobs and make lots of money, so I would advise you to go to work as soon as possible. Sam is oiling his stump now; he has got a wooden leg, but he cannot wear it long at a time yet. The company of invalids on guard at this hospital are going to be paid to day. Well, George, I guess I will lay this by till to-morrow, for I cant think of any thing more just now, besides there will probably be something turning up by to-morrow night, so good bye untill then. Friday morning, May 13th. Good morning, George, Since writing the above, I have received the tobacco it was brought to me yesterday afternoon, so you need not see George Butts about it. I am going down town to get a violin string, in a few minutes. We had one of our concerts last night; we had a fiddle, banjo, guitar, and one viol; had our concert where we always do. On the porch. The Government wagons are just going down town to work, there are about 100 of them, they go down every morning and come back every evening. I have not seen the Jones's boys in about a week, guess I shall go and see them to-day. Here comes our wench again to burn coffee. I wrote to Jim Bowman about two weeks ago, have not heard from him yet. George, I will give you a description of my room; see how you like it. It is about two thirds as large as your school room, and has three large windows, two of them open on the porch.

Letter to George ... May 12th 1864

We just open the windows and step on the porch. There are seven beds in the room, several pictures, a clock, looking glass, combs and brushes, wash stand, towel rack, spittoon, and rocking chair and three others, one large kerosene lamp, and plenty of books, besides various other little things. We have two mattresses on each bed, one hair and one husk, except mine; I have three hair ones on mine, and a good feather pillow. How do you like it? Don't you think we are comfortable enough. I have to see that the floors are all scrubbed twice a week, and the windows washed, and have the house kept in order. Last night two little boys, Doc Wilhelon and Charley West had a fight; I let them go at it till they commenced chewing each other, Then I parted them. Doc is only your size, and plays the guitar, fiddle and banjo. When we play together he plays the guitar, Johnny Johannes plays the banjo, and Doc's brother in law the base viol. Sometimes we go in the neighbors and the girls will join with the piano. Well George, I guess I will manage to worry out a letter after all. I must close now and get my string for tonight.
So good bye for a while. Give my love to Mother and all the rest. Write again next week.

From your Brother
Wm. H. Skinner

We just open the windows, and step out on the porch. There are seven beds in the room, several pictures, a clock, looking glass, combes and brushes, wash-stand, towel rack, spittoons, one rocking chair and three others, one large kerosene lamp, and plenty of books, besides various other little things. We have two mattresses on each bed, one hair and one husk, except mine; I have three hair ones on mine, and a good feather pillow. How do you like it? Don't you think we are comfortable enough. I have to see that the floors are all scrubbed twice a week, and the windows washed, and have the house kept in order. Last night two little boys, Doc Wilhelm and Charley West, had a fight; I let them go it till they commenced chewing each other, then I parted them. Doc is only your size, and plays the guitar, fiddle, and banjo. When we play together he plays the guitar, Johnny Johannes plays the banjo, and Doc's brother in law the bass viol. Sometimes we go in the neighbors and the girls will join with the piano. Well George, I guess I will manage to worry out a letter after all. I must close now and go down and get my strong, for to night. So good bye for a while. Give my love to Mother and all the rest. Write again next week.

From your Brother

Wm. H. Skinner

Letter to Hattie ... May 26th 1864

Jarvis U. S. A. General Hospital
Baltimore, Md.   May 26th 1864

Dear Sister

Your letter was received day before yesterday; glad to hear you are all well; cannot complain myself. Has been raining all the morning, and had every appearance of continuing so the rest of the day. Received a letter from John Olfee since he was here to see me. Shall not write to New York again; cannot get a word from anyone there. What is the matter with George? Time I was getting a letter from him. How does Bill Olive and Mary Cutting get along? Do they go up town to church every evening?

How are Allen's folks, and Halls, Mapes, Jone's, & everybody else? I had almost forgotten that I had promised to write to anybody but my own folks. Tell Mrs. Roworth she may look for a letter as soon as you send me her address. The rain is coming down now just as if it would not have another chance this summer. Wonder where George and Henry are today? Tell George to write all the news he can think of next time he writes, sixteen sheets full. The boys want me to go for a pitcher of ice cream, but they will have to wait till it stops raining a little; the saloon is only three squares below, quite handy; the boys buy three or four quarts every day; only five besides myself in this room now. Just opposite the saloon is Franklin Square; nearly every evening Walter & I and somebody else, take a promenade through the square,

Jarvis U.S.A. General Hospital,
Baltimore Md. May 21st 1864.

Dear Sister,

Your letter was received day before yesterday; glad to hear you are all well; cannot complain myself. Has been raining all the morning, and has every appearance of continuing so the rest of the day. Received a letter from John Lee since he was here to see me. Shall not write to New York again; cannot get a word from any one there. What is the matter with George? Time I was getting a letter from him. How does Bill Alive and Mary Cutting get along? Do they go to church every evening?

How are Allen's folks, & Halls, Whipps, Jones, & every body else? I had almost forgotten that I had promised to write to anybody but my own folks. Tell Miss Howorth she may look for a letter as soon as you send me her address. The rain is coming down now just as if it would not have another chance this summer. Wonder where George & Henry are to-day? Tell George to write all the news he can think of next time he writes, sixteen sheets full. The boys want me to go for a pitcher of ice-cream, but they will have to wait till it stops raining a little; the saloon is only three squares below, quite handy; the boys buy three or four quarts every day; only five besides myself in this room now. Just opposite the saloon is Franklin Square; nearly every evening Walter & I, and somebody else, take a promenade through the square.

Letter to Hattie ... May 26th 1864

and over to the saloon. Walter is a first rate fellow; good looking too. We always go together when we go at all, in fact, when one of us happened to be seen without the other, the first question asked is, where is your shadow? You would be surprised to hear how often the advantages of Leap Year have been taken with us, and with young ladies of the best families, but I shan't tell you. I am waiting for Evelyn, don't know if it is any of your business who Walter is waiting for. Tell Mother that I would be very glad to receive about five dollars if she can send it; my boots are played completely out, and I can not get others because they kept nearly all my pay for transportation. Will do the same the next payday for my last furlough. As soon as Evelyn and I are married I will return it. No more at present. My love to Mother and all the rest.

From your Brother
Wm. H Skinner

and over to the saloon. Walter is a first rate fellow, good looking, too. We always go together, when we go at all, in fact, when one of us happens to be seen without the other, the first question asked is, where is your shadow. You would be surprised to hear how often the advantages of Leap year have been taken with us, and with young ladies of the best families, but I shan't tell you. I am waiting for Evelyn; don't know as it is any of your business who Walter is waiting for. Tell Mother that I would be very glad to receive about five dollars if she can send it, my boots are played completely out, and I cannot get others because they kept nearly all my pay for transportation, will do the same next pay day for my last furlough. As soon as Evelyn & I are married I will return it. No more at present. My love to Mother and all the rest. From your Brother

Wm. H. Skinner.

Letter to Sister ... June 15th, 1864

Jarvis Hospital   June 15, 64

Dear Sister.

Your kind and welcome letter was received yesterday evening; was pleased to that you was enjoying good health. I am very well myself. Am going to start for my regiment Friday; expected to go yesterday, but did not get off; have not told Mother that I was going; shall not until we get there. Jim Bowman is not wounded as I was informed; he is with the Regiment, and is all right. There is about one hundred of us going together, so I will not be lonesome. We will get there just in time to get to Richmond. When you write direct the same as before and they will be forwarded to me. If you don't do as I ask you to I shall not write to you again. No more this time.

From your Brother
Wm. H Skinner

Jarvis Hospital. June 15, 64

Dear Sister,

Your kind and welcome letter was received yesterday evening; was pleased to hear that you was enjoying good health. I am very well myself. Am going to start for my Regiment friday; expected to go yesterday, but did not get off; have not told Mother that I was going; shall not untill we get there. Jim Bowman is not wounded as I was informed; he is with the Regiment, and is all right. There is about one hundred of us going together, so I will not be lonesome. We will get there just in time to get into Richmond. When you write direct the same as before and they will be forwarded to me. If you don't do as I asked you to I shall not write to you again. No more this time

From Your Brother

Wm L Skinner

Letter to Mother ... June 20th 1864

Camp Distribution
Alex. Va. June 20, 64

Dear Mother.

  Here I am on my way to my Regiment at last. Left Baltimore Friday afternoon; arrived in Washington same night at 8 O'clock; left for this camp next morning at ten o'clock; arrived here just in time for dinner, and here we have been until the present time. When we leave here (which we expect to do every day) we will bring up at the Regiment.
  We had about 40 "darks" along; when we got into our quarters at Washington, we had great sport with them; got them dancing and singing. Met some of our boys here. Weather is splendid. I will get there just in time to go into Richmond. Don't wait until you hear from me again. Do not worry on my account; I can take care of myself. No more at present.
  My love to all.
  From your son.
  Wm H Skinner

P.S. When you write to Hattie, tell her not to write till she hears from me.

Camp Distribution
Alex. Va. June 20th/64

Dear Brother,

Here I am on [crossed out: Washington] [crossed out: last Sat at Baltimore] Friday afternoon, arrived up the Chesapeake Bay Friday night at 6 oclock, left for this evening next morning at ten oclock, arrived here just in time for dinner and here we have been until the present time. When we leave here or where we expect to stay every day we will wind up at the Regiment. We had about 40 Sailors along when we got into our quarters at Washington, we had great sport with them, at them dancing and singing,

[page 2]

first some of our boys here. Everthing is prepared I will get there just in time to [crossed out] Richmond Sut I can tell any of myself no more at present. My love to all.

from your Son
Wm J. Horner

[crossed out] If you have got any money send I am not worry my account to more at present.

P.S. When you write to Sophia tell her not to write till she hears from me.

Letter to Mother ... July 23rd 1864

Camp 108th N. Y. V.   July 23/64

Dear Mother,

Received your last kind letter day before yesterday; could not answer it till to day. We have moved our camp again since I wrote you last, had been lying about a half mile in the rear; are now in the rifle pits again. Bowman and myself tent together; we don't do anything but lay around loose; consequently we have nothing to trouble us except cooking our grub. The sanitary commission furnish us with plenty of pickles and potatoes, some tobacco & other things. There has been some right smart firing lately; Burnsides "Darks" are bound to keep pecking away at the Johnnies, & they being down on niggers, are bound to

Camp 108th N.Y.V. July 23/64

Dear Mother,

Received your last kind letter day before yesterday; could not answer it till to day. We moved our camp again since I wrote last; had been laying about a half mile in the rear; are now in the Rifle Pits again. Bouma and myself tent together; we don't do any thing but lay around loose consequently we have nothing to trouble us except cooking our grub. The Sanitary Commission furnish us with plenty of pickles and potatoes, some tobacco & other things. There has been some right smart firing lately. Burnsides' "Darks" are bound to keep pecking away at the Johnnies, & they being down on the niggers, are bound to

Letter to Mother ... July 23rd 1864

return the compliment. They have a gun in one of our forts that the boys call the Petersburg express; I never could see the point until a few days ago they sent a few shells into the city; it sounded precisley like a railroad train. The boys every time they hear it are calling for tickets for Petersburg. Those stamps you sent I gave to some that I borrowed from the boys. When you send letters to me direct them as you always did to Washington D. C. Have you ever heard anything more about George Jones whether he is dead or not? We have very good quarters here if they will only let us remain here for a while. Dont know how long they will keep me here; but the longer I stay the stiffer my leg gets. The cold nights & exposure don't agree with it.

The boys were very much amused during the Rebel Raid in Maryland, at the excitement of the Baltimoreans; received a letter from a young lady there and she said that she was so much amazed at the impudence that she didn't have time to get scared. There is nothing new to write about just now, so will have to close. Write soon.

From your son
W. H. Skinner
Co. F. 1o8th N. Y. V.
Washington D. C

return the compliment. They
have a gun in one of our forts that
the boys call the Petersburg express.
I never could see the point, until
a few days ago they sent a few
shells into the city. It sounds just
like a railroad train. The
every time they hear it one called
shots for Petersburg. Those months
sent I gave for some that I
one of the boys. When you
letters to me direct them
as always did, to Washington D.C.
if you heard anything more
of George Jones whether he is
or not? We have very good
tens now if they will only let us
remain here a while God knows
how long they will keep me here,
but the longer I stay the stiffer
my leg gets. The cold nights &
adjourns don't agree with it.

The boys were very much
amused during the Rebel Raid
in Maryland at the excitement
of the Baltimorians, required
a little from a large body
of shoes on the part of the
inhabitants who got so thoroughly
so much frightened that one
lady that she didn't have time
to get scared. She is putting
now to write about just now, I
B will have to close. Write
soon

From Morgan Jones
                Washington D.C.

Letter to Hattie ... August 28th 1864

City Point Hospital
August 28th 1864

Dear Sister

You have probably wondered why I have neglected to write for so long; haven't you? Well, I don't wonder at it, for it is some time since I have written to you. You will perceive by this that your "salient brother" is again an inmate of the hospital. Have been here since July 29th; don't know how much longer they will keep me here; the doctor says I will never be fit for duty, but still they hang on to me.

I received a letter from home a few days ago, and sent one in reply; folks were all well. Jim Bowman is with the regiment. When I left the Regt. one month ago, there were forty nine men left; since then they have been engaged several times, and several have

City Point Hospital
August 28th 1864

Dear Sister,

You have probably wondered why I have neglected to write for so long, haven't you? Well, I don't wonder at it, for it is some time since I have written to you. You will discover by this that your absent brother is an inmate of the hospital. Have been here since July 24th; don't know how much longer they will keep me here; the doctor says I will never be fit for duty, but still they will hang on to me.

I received a letter from home a few days ago, and sent one in reply; folks were all well. Jim Bowman is with the regiment. When I left the Regt. one month ago, there were forty nine men left; since then they have been engaged several times, and several have

Letter to Hattie ... August 28th 1864

been taken sick; consequently, there cannot be many of them left; at that note there will not be a shadow of a Regiment left next August.

I hear very often from my friends in Baltimore; wish I was there now; it was my own fault that I came here, and no one but myself is to blame for it, so I shall not growl.

The patients in the hosp. are very well cared for; the Christian Commission is doing a great deal for the welfare of the soldiers; but there is none from New York. There was one N. Y. establishment here some time ago; they had two clay pipes on hand until one of the boys got them, and then they shut up shop. George Jones is either dead or a prisoner. One of the Regt. who new the boys, told me that he was wounded badly, but don't know what became of him.

There is a boat going to leave here for Philadelphia tomorrow with sick and wounded. I may be sent away with the rest, so I would not advise you to write; but if you don't hear from me very soon, you may rest assured that I am safe enough for they will not send me to the Regt.

I presume while I am writing this, that you are enjoying a tete-a-tete with some of the young ladies of Fairport, or perhaps with one of the Beaux. Give my love to all the pretty girls in Fairport. Guess I will close this now.

From your
Brother
Wm. H Skinner

"There is a boat going to leave here for Philadelphia tomorrow with sick and wounded, I may be sent away with the rest, so I would not have time to write; but if you don't hear from me very soon, you may rest assured that I am safe enough, for they will not permit me to tell you I presume while I am writing this, that you are very uneasy a tête-à-tête with some of still young Lord of Fairport, or perhaps with of the Beau-Ton My Dear, I'm Mortts good in Fairport Guess I will close this now

Yours

Mr. J. Skinner."

has been taken prisoner amongst them, doesn't it miss of them left, at that rate there would not be a shadow of us by next August I have put by next August I have dog after dog my friend in Kitchen, and I what I have, not there's no par — paper that I know of, and my own spill infamous and my own but myself. to blame for this I shall not grow the patience of this Soph to enflame my Soph are very well and for the Christian Experiences going is not feel at all the welfare of this Soph: but there is enough among the Blue Cap's there and on The Establishment here some time ago, they had two Spy tribes on hand until one of the trigs got them, and then they shut up shop. George Sons is either dead or a prisoner. One of the Reg't. who knew the boys, told me that he was wounded badly, but doesn't know what became of him.

Letter to Mother ... September 17th 1864

Douglas Hospital
Washington, D. C.
Sept. 17ʰ 1864

Dear Mother

I sent you a letter a few days ago; have received no reply yet, maybe because it is not time; no mater, shall try it again, for it is awful dull here.

I never knew what it was to be in jail before coming to this hospital; one cannot hardly get a glimpse out of doors with out a pass. We are in a large brick building – three of them being together – which composes the main portion of the hospt. the other portion being barracks, and the whole surrounded by a brick wall eight feet high.

I have been out on pass twice since coming here. Went through the capital yesterday; saw all that was worth seeing. As for the city, there is not money enough in it to tempt me to live in it. Baltimore is far ahead of it. After going through the capital, I got into a street car and rode Penna. Avenue some distance; but I was more astonished and disgusted during that short ride than ever I was. There were eight or ten niggers of both sexes seated with the rest; one big black rascal between two white women; all mixed like pepper and salt. But to top off with, when the

Douglas Hospital
Washington D.C.
Sept 17th 1864

Dear Brother,

I received your kind
letter a few days ago, and
was really glad, though I was
not long, no matter, I shall
again for it is awful dull here.
I never knew such an
to be any fun for anyone in
the hospital, men are dying
got no exemption now, but I
hope of half those who
are dying they must
be together, and they happen
they main portions of this place
the other portion being made
by the whole surrounded by a

brick wall eight feet high.
I have been out on pass
twice since coming here.
Went through the Capitol
yesterday, saw all that was
worth seeing. As for the
City of Washington it is not much
of to compare with Phila[delphia].
Baltimore is far ahead of it.
After going through the
Capitol, I got onto a street car
and rode Pennsylvania Avenue
its whole distance, but was agreeably
disappointed during that short
ride then expected was.
There you would
see negroes, little ones and
with their mothers, big sisters,
(and between the white
women), all hugging every
happen, all negro styling
like people and daily but
to top it off with, sometimes

Letter to Mother ... September 17th 1864

car was full. There were four young girls (white) got in and were obliged to stand up, and look at the dirty ragged, greasy contrabands enjoying themselves. I was once an admirer of the Abe, but now am heartily ashamed of it, and have been for some time; I would soon cut my throat than vote for him.

The officials in Washington are working hard among the soldiers for Lincoln.. Some of them probably will sell themselves for the sake of a furlough, but I think the majority in this city are for little Mac. At the front I know they are nearly all for McClellan. If I had a hundred votes to give, Little Mac should have all and they might keep their furloughs and discharges to light their cigars with.

The doctor tried to straighten my leg this morning but did not succeed. Write soon.

From your
Son
Wm H Skinner
Douglas Hospt.
Washington D. C.
Ward 4, Bed 152

eye was full, there were
four young guys (white) got
in and were obliged to stand
up, and look at the ugly,
ragged, greasy contrabands
enjoying themselves. I was
busily employed in studying
have seen for some time. I found
some ough my thread than the ground
The niggers in Washington
are surpising many they formerly
for I imagine Some of them forget they
will fully themselves to the state of a
few days ago. I think the manner
in which they are pushed about
the front I show they are fully
able for Mc.Clellan. If I. C
had a hundred guides of my
little Mac. Should he lack for
and they might keep their
fur coughs and discharges to

right there begans with
ing doctor there is
through ten my leg this mor-
ing but and rheumatized thrie
days. My love to all.
From John

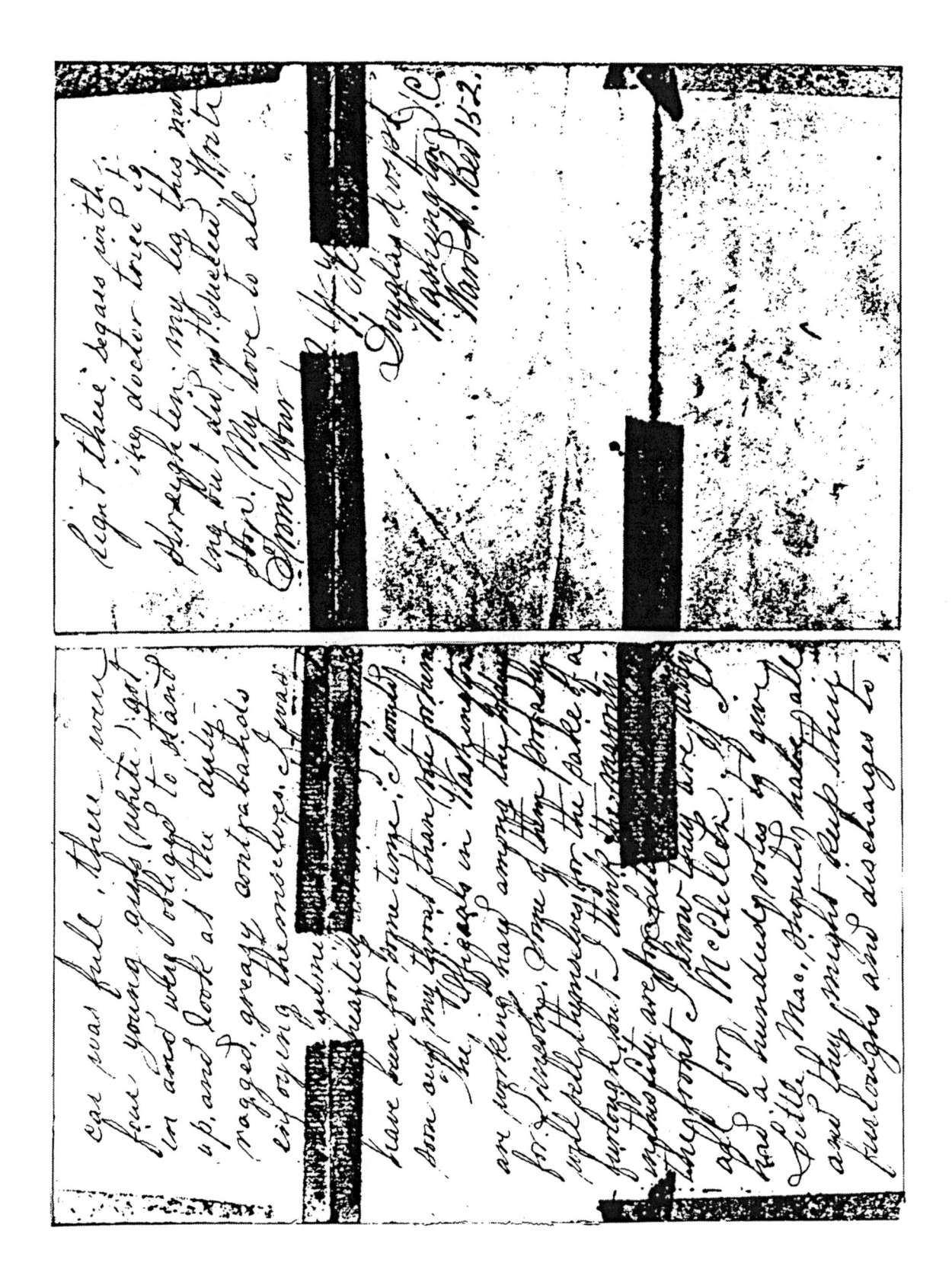

Duggles Nurse
Newburg, N.C.
March 4th 1862.

Letter to Hattie ... October 6th 1864

Douglas Hospital
Washington D.C.
Oct. 6th 1864

Dear Sister

I received a couple of papers from you today, was very glad to get them if they were old. It is very lonesome here, and they will help pass a little of the time away. It is now nearly 12 o'clock P.M.. We have a night watch and I have to take my turn with the rest, and if the patients want anything, to wait on them.
Tell John Olmstead that I wish him much joy and all sorts of good luck; and tell him that that was the first

Douglas Hospital
Washington D.C.
Oct 5th 1864.

Dear Sister,
I received a couple of papers from you to-day; was very glad to get them if they were old. It is very lonesome here, and they will help pass a little of the long away. It is now nearly 12 o'clock P.M. We have a night watch and I have to take my turn with the rest, and if the patients want anything to wait on them.

Tell John Olmsted that I wish him much joy and all sorts of good luck, and tell him that that was the first

[envelope addressed to:]
Hattie E. Skinner
Hanford's Landing
16 Hattie Monroe Co
N.Y.

Letter to Hattie ... October 6th 1864

chew of good tobacco I've had since I left Baltimore.

I had a letter from George today. We have any quantity (number) of sisters of charity at the Hospital, and they are the greatest nuisance out of jail, but I might as well said in jail, for I can compare this place is nothing else. They are allways bothering around and disturbing the men.

Are both John and Bill living at the landing now? How does Bill Olive and his wife get along? Who else is going to make fools of themselves and get married? I must hurry and finish writing this for I am hungry and have seven or eight slices of bread & butter to demolish.

There is a Brigadier Genl. a Captain and several Lets. in a ward I am in. We are on second floor of a dwelling house, same as I was at Balti. and although it is a much handsomer building, it is not near so nice a place as we had in Baltimore. I must quit now for want of something to write.

From your brother
W H Skinner
Ward 3

hear of good tobaco for his
since I left Baltimore.
I had a letter from
George today. He have any
quantity (number) of Pistols
though as the Hospital, and
they are the greatest nuisance
out of jail, but it might as
well be said in jail for I
can compare this place to
nothing else. They are all
very bothering, noisy and
slovering set. I am Bill
L___ the both John and Bill
dying at the Boarding ___
yonder days Bill Clark and
his wife get along. They
are so going to make ____ of
I thimbelord and get manues. I
thought Henry and finished hunting
this for I am hungry and have

dung or eight hives of
bees & billy to dembish.
There is a Garden ___
of Baltimore and generally
in the war. I ___. ___
are a front ___ of a ___
brings ___ as hips at Buffs
and although I was much
and ___ buildings is not
near the price a ___ as ___ as
in Baltimore. I must quit
now for want of something
to write.
from your brother
H. H. Skinner
Ward 8

Letter to Lucy ... October 21st 1864

Douglas Hosp.
Oct 21 / 64

Dear Sister

Yours of the 16th not coming to hand this morning; have nothing to do just at present so I will answer it. Don't know as I shall make out much of a letter this time for it is impossible to find anything new in this place. However I shall try what can be done in that line.

To commence with the weather is delightfull; has been so with the exception of a few days past which were rather cool but yesterday opened bright and warm.

Received a letter from Mother yesterday. Says she is going home soon.

I saw Col. Rivers of my Regt. A few days ago. He was here to see General Conner. By the way Lucy, I must tell you about my patients I am nursing in 3rd ward. We have Genl. Conner, Captain Briseve and three Lieutenants, besides several Privates. The Genl. can't get out of bed nor even turn on his side on account of his wound, which is very severe. I help to dress it every day. I live

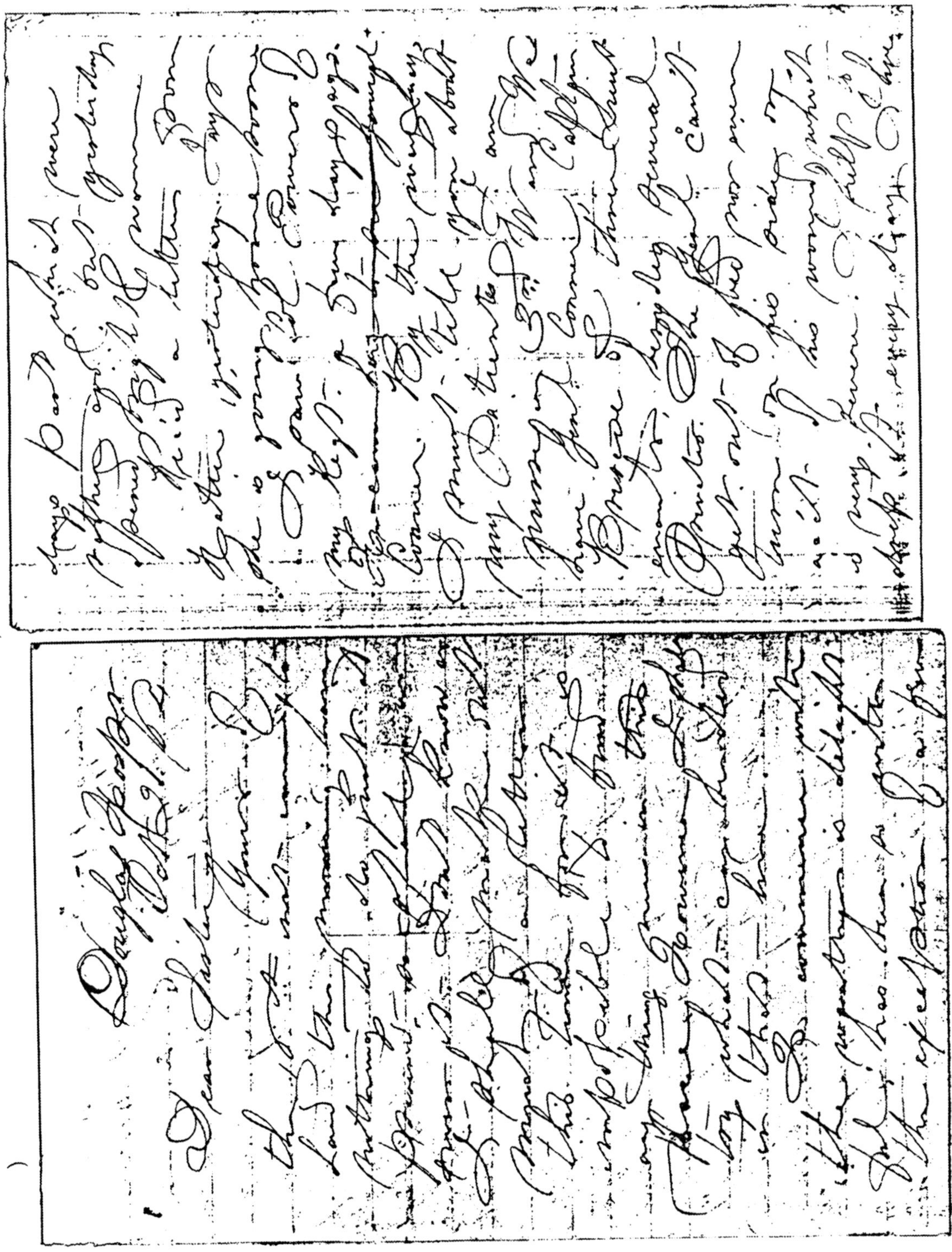

Letter to Lucy ... October 21st 1864

tip top now. The officers pay a dollar a day each for their meals & I have a share in it. There is a little French man here who plays the flute to perfection & two who play the guitars. We have plenty of music. We have also a melodeon & if I stay here long shall have a violin.

    I am sorry the young married folks are so unfortunate at the landing but I don't know as it troubles me as I don't intend to bother any of the landing ladies myself.. When my time is out I am going to Constantinople or some other good place for a wife. No more at present. My respects to all.

From your Brother
Will

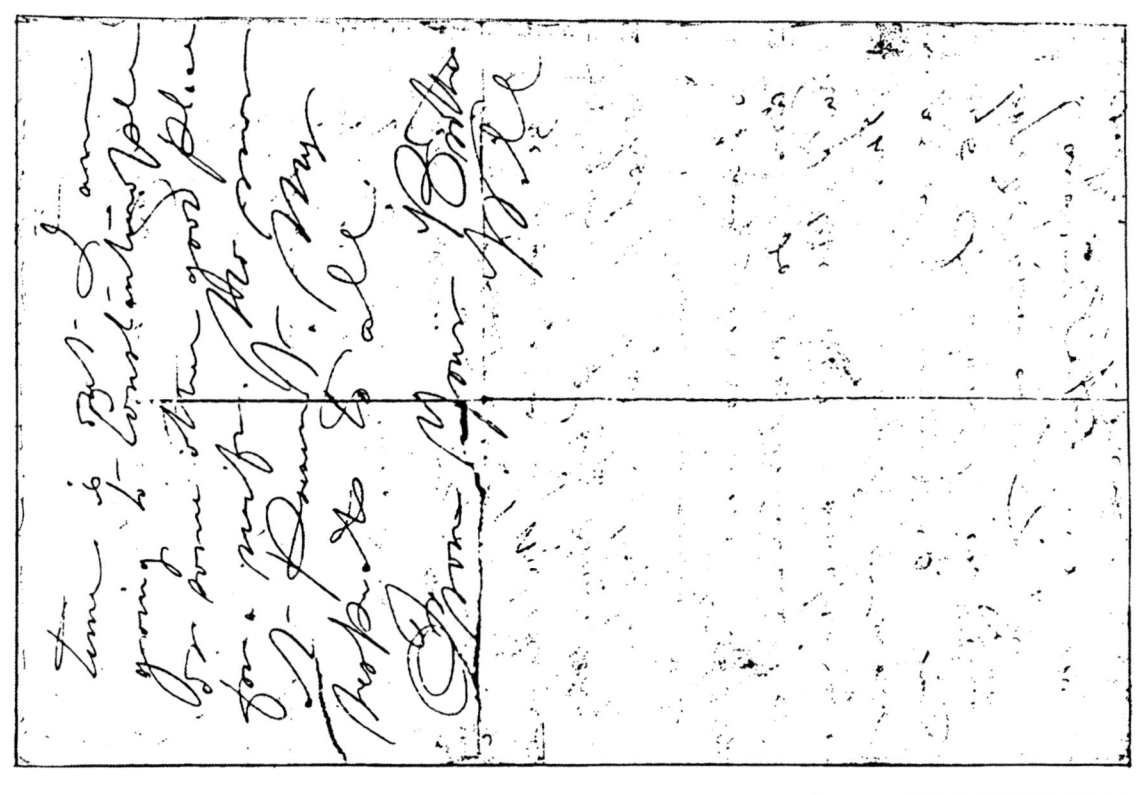

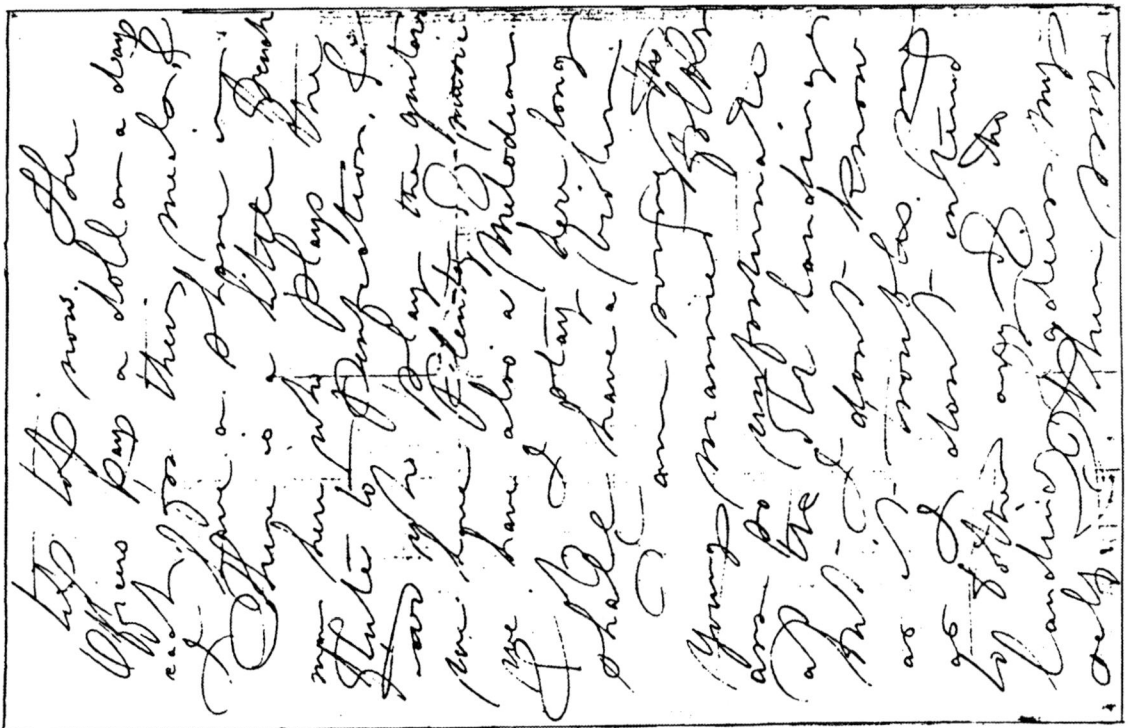

| S | 108 | N.Y. |

William Skinner

Pvt., Co. F, 108 Reg't N. Y. Infantry.

Appears on

Company Muster Roll

for Sept & Oct, 1864.

Present or absent: Absent

Stoppage, $_____ 100 for _____

Due Gov't, $_____ 100 for _____

Remarks: Sick at U.S. Gen'l Hospital

Book mark:

E. B. Thompson
(858)   Copyist.

| S | 108 | N.Y. |

Wm. Skinner

Pvt., Co. F, 108 Reg't N.Y.V.

Appears on

Hospital Muster Roll

of Douglas U. S. A. General Hospital,

at Washington, D. C.,

for Sept & Oct, 1864.

Attached to hospital:

When Sept. 9, 1864.

How employed _____

Last paid by Maj. _____

to _____, 186 .

Bounty paid $_____ 100; due _____ 100

Present or absent: Present

Remarks _____

Book mark: _____

G. W. _____

To all whom it may concern:

The bearer hereof _W. Skinner_ _Priv_ of Company _"F"_ Company of the _108th_ Regiment of _New York Vol_ aged _23_ years, _5' 9"_ inches high, _fair_ completion _blue_ eyes, _light_ hair, and by profession a _Farmer_ ; born in the State of _N. Y._ and enlisted at _Rochester_ in the _State_ of _N. Y._ on the _6th_ day of _Aug_ eighteen hundred and _62_ to serve for the period of _3 years_, is permitted to go to _Rochester_, in the County of _Monroe_, State of _N. Y._, he having received a FURLOUGH from the _4th_ day of _Nov._ to the _16th_ day of _Nov 1864_, at which period he will rejoin ~~his Company regiment at~~ _Douglas Hosp_ ~~or wherever it then may be~~, OR BE CONSIDERED A DESERTER.

Subsistence has been furnished to said _W. Skinner_, to the _4th_ day of _Nov_, and pay to the ___ day of _____, both inclusive.

Given under my hand at _Washington D. C._ this _4th_ day of _Nov._, 18_64_.

Wm. F. Danis
Asst. Surg. U.S.A.

Douglas Hospt.

To all whom it may Concern.

Extract from Army Regulations, edition 1861.

Par. 130..Furloughs will be granted only by the commanding officer of the post, or the commanding officer of the regiment actually quartered with it. Furloughs may be prohibited at the discretion of the officer in command.
Par. 131..Soldiers on furlough shall not take with them their arms or accoutrements.

The bearer hereof, W. Skinner Priv of Capt's "F" Company of the 105 Regiment of New York Vols aged 23 years, 5 feet 9 inches high, fair complexion, blue eyes, light hair, and by profession a Farmer; born in the State of N.Y. and enlisted at Rochester in the State of N.Y. on the 6 day of Aug eighteen hundred and 62, to serve for the period of 3 years, is hereby permitted to go to Rochester in the County of Monroe, State of N.Y., he having received a FURLOUGH from the 4 day of Nov to the 16 day of Nov 1864, at which period he will rejoin his Company or regiment at Douglas Hosp or wherever it then may be, OR BE CONSIDERED A DESERTER.

Subsistence has been furnished to said W. Skinner to the 4 day of Nov and pay to the ___ day of ___, both inclusive.

Given under my hand, at Washington D.C. this 4 day of Nov 1864

Wm. F. Norris
Asst Surg U.S.A.
Commanding the Reg't

Douglas Hosp.

[A.G.O. No. 16 & Pl. 1]

Letter to Mother ... December 18th 1864

*Douglas Hospt.
Dec. 18 1864*

Dear Mother

I received a letter yesterday from George & Martha, & a few lines from you. You spoke of my not having written since I left home so thought I would now. George said you was sick. I am very sorry to hear that. I hope you will be well soon. For myself, I have not known yet what it is to be sick. But I presume my time will come some day. Nevertheless, I am entirely ruined for any kind of

Douglas Hospt.
Dec. 18th /64

Dear Mother,

letter ~~[struck out]~~
& Martha, & a few lines
from you. You spoke of
my not having written
to you since I left home
so thought I would ~~[struck]~~
George said you was sick.
am very sorry to hear that
& hope you will be well very
soon. For myself, I have
not known yet what it is
to be sick. But I presume
my time will come some
day. Nevertheless, I am entirely ruined for any kind of

Letter to Mother ... December 18th 1864

laborious work. I have been transferred to the Vet. Reserve Corps; consequently will remain here until my time is out. But at what a cost. I am ruptured so badly I can't chop a stick of wood. Delightful prospect for a young man without a home or trade by which he could earn his grub. Well there is no one to blame but myself, if I had staid in Baltimore twould not have been. The Doctor says twas the strain on one leg to favor the other that caused it. There is one thing, however I can do. Am fond of writing & can write a pretty good hand (though I don't always do it). I can go to clerking, or traveling on the little wit I posses.

George & Martha are wishing for Christmas presents. I can't hardly get tobacco I want, so they will see I can't send them anything. Wish George would go a few months to that teacher & learn the music. Have hated myself many a time because I did not pay more attention to it. Is Hattie at Fairport now? There is nothing more I can think of so will close with love to you & all.

From
Your Son
Wm. H. S.

glorious work. Have the little nut of hofses.
been transferred to the George & Martha are waiting
Bet. Reserve lots, consequently for Christmas forwards. I can't
will remain here until my hardly get tobacco I want &
time is out. But at what a they tell me 9 cant get them
_____ _____ pu daddy any thing. Well
_____ _____ of good. _____ a few months cause of
Delightful prospect for a I heard the squire. Have hall
young man without a home myself many a time because of
by trade by which he could earn did not pay more attention to
his eat. Well there is no it. So Lottie at Fairport now?
one to blame but myself. If I There is nothing more I can
had played in Baltimore I would think of so will close with
not have been. The Doctor says love to you & all.
lings the strain on one leg to stand
the other that caused it. There Your Son Wm H. D.
is one thing however I can do
Am fond of writing & can
write a pretty good hand (I think)
I don't always blot) I can go
to sticking, or traveling on

Card 1

S | 108 | N.Y.

W. Skinner

Pvt., Co. F, 108 Reg't N. Y. Infantry.

Appears on Regimental Return

for November, 186 4

Present or absent Absent

Gain or loss .... , 186

Date .... , 186 .

Place ....

Remarks: Sick

NEXT RETURN ON FILE FEB 1865

Book mark: ....

R. J. Hunt

Card 2

S | 108 | N.Y.

Wm Skinner

Pvt., Co. F, 108 Reg't N. Y. Infantry.

Appears on Company Muster Roll

for Nov & Dec, 1864

Present or absent Absent

Stoppage, $ .... 100 for ....

Due Gov't, $ .... 100 for ....

Remarks: In U.S.A. Genl Hospital

Book mark: ....

E. B. Thompson, Capt.

(368)

Card 3

S | 108 | N.Y.

William Skinner

Pvt., Co. F, 108 Reg't N. Y. V.

Appears on Hospital Muster Roll

of Douglas U. S. A. General Hospital,
Washington, D. C.

at Nov & Dec, 1864

for ....

Attached to hospital: Sep 1, 1864

When ....

How employed ....

Last paid by Maj. Gates

to Nov 31, 1864.

Bounty paid $ .... 100; due $ ......

Present or absent Transfd to V.R.C. Dec 27/64

Remarks: ....

Book mark: ....

G. W. Chase

Letter to Mother ... January 1st 1865

Douglas Hospital
Jan 1st 1865

Dear Mother,

Your kind letter was recieved this morning and as it's rather dull this evening, thought I could not occupy my time better than in writing you a letter. This has been a dull New Years; if we had not had plenty of visitors I don't know how we would have passed the day. However it has passed and it is now 7 o'clock. We have a rousing fire of pine logs in the fire place, which makes it quite cheerful! By the way, Mother, if ever I should get married (which is not very likely), I shall have a fireplace for my own special benefit. Talking of getting married reminds me of some thing I have been thinking of lately; that it would be a good idea for me to run away with some rich old fellows daughter; don't you think it would?

But Mother, by the tone of your letter I infer that you think I am a poor miserable cripple and would be so as long as I live! You must not let any such notion as that worry you; for it is not so. I am only rendered unfit for hard work. I have full use of my limbs; only in walking far I become tired. Don't worry on my account Mother. I will get along right smart.

Don't think about presents for me Mother, think of what you need yourself; you understand me. I don't need anything more than I can get here. Besides it is high time (as Father

Douglas Hospital
Jan 14/15

Dear Brother

Your kind letter was received this morning & is its nature dull this evening thought I can't post receipt of my being better than I am sending you a letter this day. I don't sent to New Year. If you had read that plenty of visiting I don't ask that friends to visit my people. Anyone here I would have perhaps left day. If every of this before it is away I enjoy it. My other is having fun. If I have dogs in the few places I would make it quite cheerful. By the way, My other (never I think) and praying (which is not my liking), I shall have a fine place for my own special

bought the thing of getting one and promised give it some thing, has been thinking of late ; that it would be a good idea for my to go away, to the some one old fellows daughter; don't you think it would?

But brother by the time of your letter I infer that you think I am a poor miserable cripple & would be so as long as I live. I'm just not bet any much notice as that every you, for if I refuse, I am only repulsed on it. If you have work. Have full use of my hands, am in nothing face I become tired. Don't worry on my account. Mother I will get along right smart.

But think about presents for me, Mother, think of what you must yourself if you understand me, I won't buy any thing, more than I can get here. Besides it is high time (as Arthur

Letter to Mother ... January 1st 1865

has often told me) for me to be looking out for myself. You know I never was afraid of work (though Father has) & I am not afraid of it now, that is, any work I am capable of doing & that I think will be to travel & see some of this world of ours, so you see Hanfords Landing will not be large enough to hold me in future.

What is the matter with Hattie & George, they don't write near so well as they used to; & such horrid spelling. Tell George I thank him for the ring, but hereafter he must take more care in finishing them.

You asked me how I fared here? We have plenty to eat, & good and not much to do at present; can do all my days work in one hour. We have a melodeon, guitar, banjo, flute, & I have a good violin; we we have plenty of music you see. I hear from Jim Bowman often. He says Hattie don't answer his letters.

Well I will bid you good night. My love to all.

Your affectionate
son
William

has the time told me for you to be looking out for myself. You know I never was afraid of work (though Father say I am not afraid of it now) that is, any work I am capable of doing & that I think I will be able to travel & see some of this part of our possessions that I one day hope to hold until not for days enough to hold me off future.

That is the matter with Hattie & George. They don't write you so oft as they ought to & once I heard Nelly tell Pop I guess they out him for the ring, but Hula flew the quest have made me in throwing the eat.

They asked me (how I was) and we have plenty to eat I God; and not much to do at present, exp ag all my days work in our hopi. We have a Melodeon, Guitar, banjo flute, & I have a good violin; for have plenty of Music you see.

I hear from Jim Bowman often. He says Hattie don't answer his Letters. Well I must bid you good night.—May Love to all.

Your affectionate
Son William.

Letter to Lucy ... March 28th 1865   **No original letter**

Douglas Host.
Mar 28th 65

Dear Lucy

Your kind letter of the 25th is just received, and most welcome it was I assure you. But I was very sorry to learn that Mrs. Roworth has been so ill, for she is one of a few kind friends I am fortunate enough to have. I hope she will recover speedily. You must take the best care of her.

You speak of my not writing to you for so long. Did I not in my last letter mention something about the Hospt. being broken up soon? It strikes me very forcibly that I did, and that I told you not to look for a letter soon. We have been expecting it every day, but we have not vamoosed the ranch yet. I presume we poor will be scattered all around. I hope they will keep the company together and not separate us, but wot's the hods as long's your 'appy?

So you are acquainted with Mr. John Goodyear and lady? Very glad to hear it. My compliments to them. Will be happy to accept their invitation if I go home. Ask John if he ever learned anything of George Peacock. I hardly think it would answer for me to write to them first, but will answer all letters I may receive with pleasure.

What the duce do you mean by having a _____ to support? Do you mean a horse, a dog, or a moustache? If the later, you are about right; there would be no chance for anything else. But I don't happen to have a weakness in that direction, consequently, I am not a possessor of one of those necessary appendages.

When Mother gets home be sure to tell her to write to me immediately. Is Bill Caudle living in Rochester now? What is he doing?

The review was a splendid sight; I saw the whole of it. The weather was beautiful and everything was in excellent trim for the occasion. I saw the 108th; spoke to Sergt. Anger but could not to all. The regt. Looks well; the boys all had a smile on their countenance.

I am going to see that young lady to-night if every thing goes happens and nothing goes wrong.

Well goodbye Lucy. Remember me to all

Your Brother.
W. H. S.

Letter to Mother ... April 10th 1865

Douglas Hospt.
April 10th/65

Dear Mother

You have not answered my last letter yet, but I thought I would write again to keep in practice, though the practice will not be very beneficial for I have a game thumb and cannot hold the pen with it, so I have to hold it between my fingers.

We received the news of the surrender of Gen. Lee and his army last night; everything goes bravely on; guess the rebels

Douglas Hospt.
April 10th/65.

Dear Brother,
You have not answered my last letter yet but I thought I would write again to keep in practice; though the practice will not be very beneficial for I have a game thumb and cannot hold the pen with it, so I have to hold it between my fingers.

We received the news of the surrender of Gen Lee and his army last night: every thing goes bravely on: guess the rebels

Letter to Mother ... April 10th 1865

can be whipped in four or five years, if old Abe tries right smart. Too bad to disappoint the northern copperheads aint it. Too bad that the greenbacks could not become worthless too, so as not to disappoint them too bad the war could not last four years longer to humor them. Well I hope they will get their eyes opened one of these days.

Why don't somebody write to me occasionally? I don't get a letter once a fortnight. I have received no letter from Mrs. Fillmore.

Well, Mother, August will soon be around again and I will be loose again. Oh if I only had a decent education, I would ask for nothing else to start with. Do not even know enough to fill the commonest book-keepers position.

Well I shall not cry over it, but just for fun I would like some fortune teller to inform me how I am going to earn my potatoes. How handy it would come now if some sick uncle would only kick the bucket and leave me a fortune, or if I could only strike oil. What is going on at the Landing – anything new? Anybody there wants to hire a man to work on farm? If there are please recommend me. Well good bye Mother.
My love to all the family.

Your affectionate son
WHS

can be supplied in four or five years if not are frugright small. too bad to disappoint the mother Blockheads ain't it? too bad that the Quenknobs could not become soon tilers too, so as not to disappoint them too bad the war could not last four years longer to humor them. Well, I hope they will yet, they eyes opened one of these days. Why don't somebody send to me reasonably. I don't get a letter once a fortnight. I have received no letter from Mr. Fillmore since Mother August will you be among agony. And I will be love again. If I only had a decent education I could get something else to plant with. Do not even know enough to fill the commonest of the offices position well I shall not try out it, but

that for me, I would like some inform letter to inform me how I am going to earn my bread. Ebra nobody will concern myself Some pork uncle would only kick the bucket and leave one of them. If I could only strike it. What is going on at the landing anything great. Any body then robin to him a man to rent a farm. If there are please remember me. Well good bye Mother. My love made the family.

Your affectionate Mrs.

Letter to Lucy ... April 20th 1865   **No original letter**

Douglas Hospital
April 20,65

Dear Lucy,

Yours was received yesterday morning with one from Mother, and nothing from Hattie. Was much pleased to receive such a nice long letter. It was the longest one I have received in an age; don't know Lucy if I can give you as long a one or not. I do not feel like writing just now; the only feeling I have now is for vengeance on the cowardly traitors who caused the murder of our president. Wrote to Mother this morning.

I saw the funeral procession yesterday. There is nothing of interest to write at present but the murder and funeral and that you will learn more about from the papers than I can tell you.

Am glad to hear such a flattering account as you gave me of the people of Rochester. I have entertained a poor opinion of the city since I was home and a poorer one of the town of Greece. Hope it was a mistaken opinion as regards the city, but I have no hope for the other.

I went to the capital this afternoon and saw the President's remains; he looks almost the same as when I saw him last. The rain has been pouring down hard all day; but it didn't keep back those who were anxious to see him.

How many times I have wished for power to bring him back to life again. How often have I wished for a chance to torture the miserable, cowardly wretch that murdered him. But his time will come; men will not be wanting to seek from one end of the world to the other to find him. The soldiers are crazy; were they to get hold of the coward, he would soon get his due.

I received that book you sent. I leave you to read those lines I sent George; you read the others so easily. Tell Hattie I cannot get those photo's just now. I will close now for the mail.

Love to all.
Your Brother.
W. H. Skinner

Letter to Hattie ... May 4th 1865

Douglas Hosp.
May 4th/65

Dear Sister

I received two letters, one from you & one from Lucy yesterday. Must answer both now & in one. The hospital is going to be broken up immediately. Do not write again until you hear from me Don't know where we will be sent yet, but as near as I can ascertain, we are going to be transferred south and be consolidated with some other company.

Douglas Hospt.
May 4th/65

Dear Sister,
I received two letters, one from you & one from Lucy yesterday. Must answer both now & in one. The Hospital is going to be broken up immediately. Do not write again until you hear from me. Don't know where we will be sent yet, but as near as I can ascertain, we are going to be transfered South and be consolidated with some other Company.

Letter to Hattie ... May 4th 1865

It will probably be two or three weeks before I can let you know where we are. Now the war is ended, there is no use of so many hospitals, and they are braking up several. I sent you the photo you wanted.

I hope we will go down as far as Charleston. Want to see that country very much. All the patients who are able to go home are going to be discharged soon as possible. Those who are not will be transferred to another Hosp. The V. R. C's will be kept. General Connor is here yet; has not been off his back in twelve months; will soon be able to get up. I have nothing to do but drink his ale & smoke his cigars for six months. Well good bye all till you hear from me again.

Your Brother
W. H. S.

You will probably be two or three nights before I can let you know where we are. Now the war is ended there is no use of so many hospitals, and they are breaking up several. I send you the photo you want Lis.

If & when we will go down as far as Charlotte I don't see that Gen'l G'ty to bring my h. All the patients who are able to go-away are going to be transferred am to Petersb. Those who are not will be trans fer'd to Annster Hosp. Fed Va. Cap. & the Rebt. Gen'l going to have ye has not-her as he took in

Pacha month I will be able to get up. I have has nothing to do but drink his ale & smoke his segars for 2 months Tell you shye all well. You hear from me again
Your Brother
W. H. L.

| 108 | N.Y.

William H. Skinner

Pvt., Co. H, 108 Reg't N. Y. Infantry.

Appears on Co. Muster-out Roll, dated

Bailey Cross Roads Va, May 28, 1865.

Muster-out to date ...., 186 .

Last paid to ...., 186 .

Clothing account:

Last settled ...., 186 ; drawn since $ 100

Due soldier $ .... 100 ; due U. S. $ 100

Am't for cloth'g in kind or money adv'd $ 100

Due U. S. for arms, equipments, &c., $ 100

Bounty paid $ .... 100 ; due $ 100

Remarks: Transferred to V.R.C. March 15, 1865

Book mark: ....

E. B. Thompson

(361)

Letter to Hattie ... June 11th 1865

Douglas Hospital
June 11th/65

Dear Sister,

I think it is about time I answered your letter; don't you? Did not expect to be here so long or it should have been answered long ago. You see we are in daily expectation of being sent away from here and cannot tell where; but it will be but a short time now till we go. The patients are being discharged as fast as possible, and Douglas Hospt. will cease to exist; and when that happens our company will leave for parts unknown at present.

Douglas Hospital.
June 11th/65.

Dear Sister.

I think it is about time I answered your letter; don't you? Did not expect to be here so long or it should have been answered long ago. You see, we are in daily expectation of being sent away from here, and cannot tell where: but it will be but a short time now till we go. The patients are being discharged as fast as possible, and Douglas Hosp'l. will cease to exist, and when that happens our Company will leave for parts unknown at present.

Letter to Hattie ... June 11th 1865

I suppose you saw the 108th when they arrived in Rochester. I didn't know they were going home until the day after they left Washington or I should have seen them. I saw them on the review, but could not speak to anyone but Sergt. Anger. What is Jim at; tell him to write to me; if we are not hear our letters will be sent to us. I don't expect to get out till my time is out.

How is Mrs. Roworth; does she get any better?

Has Mother got home yet? I wrote to aunt Ann the day after receiving your letter; have no answer yet. Has Rus Wall got home yet? I wrote to Lucy the same day; no answer yet. How does Father get along with farming this summer?

I presume you are well at home, as you said nothing to the contrary in your letter.

My health is as usual; tiptop. Sickness and I have had a falling out.

I see the 140th has been home too. What sort of a reception did the 100th have? Has Henry Jones been discharged?

Love to all –
Your Brother
Wm H Skinner

I suppose you saw the 100$ when they turned up Rochester.

I did not know they were going home until the day after they left Aurora, or I should have seen them. I saw them on the river, but could not speak to any me but Gough Boys. What is John at, let him come to me, if we are not to have our wittles we will be sent to us. I don't expect to get out yet, tell Guy time is up. Lone is my favorite, does she get any better?

Has mother got home yet? I wrote to mother to-day 4 days the play after. I received your letter have no answer yet, Gus has got safe home yet. I wrote to Guy the same day, no answer yet. How does father get along

with the farming this summer?

I presume you are well at home, as you paid nothing to the printer in your letter. My health is by no means tip top, so keep up and I have had a falling out.

Boy the 140th has gone home too. What part of a reception day the 108th have had. I envy Jones run discharges?

Write to all —
Your Brother
Wm E. Skinner

APPLICATION FOR INVALID PENSION

STATE of NEW YORK

On this 20th day of January A.D.
one thousand eight hundred and sixty six personally appeared before me
Clerk of the Monroe County Court, within and for the County and State aforesaid
William H. Skinner   age 24 years, a resident of Rochester
in the County of Monroe, in the State of New York, who being duly sworn according to law,
declares that he is the identical   William H. Skinner who enlisted in the service of
United States at Rochester, N. Y. on the eighth day of August
in the year of 1862, was a Private in Company F commanded by Captain
F. E. Pierce in the 108th Regiment of New York Volunteers in
In the war of 1861 and was honorably discharged at Douglas Hospital inx the District of Columbia
On the fifteenth day of August A. D. 1865; that while in the ser-
Vice of the United States, and in the line of his duty he received the following wound that
which is the U. S. service and in the line of his duty he was wounded
by a shell fired by the enemy at the battle of Gettysburg in
the third day of July 1863. Said shell struck him in the thigh
of the left leg carrying away part of the leg and injuring
the cords & muscles. Said wound immediately disabled him
for duty & he was carried back to field hospital and from their to
Janis Hospital Baltimore, Md. where he arrived the 14th of July 1963.
And remained there nearly eleven months during which time he was
mostly confined to his bed. He was not able to straighten his leg and
was all the time under the surgeons charge. From there he was sent
first to City Pinch Hospital where he was examined until the 8th of Sept.
1864 where his wound was again opened. He was then removed to Douglass Hospital, Washington D. C. where he remained until he was
discharged on the 15th day of August 1865. Before entering the
army he worked on a farm but is now unable to resume that occupation on account said wound. nor is he able to labor at any hard work
with his wound troubling him so much that he can hardly walk.
Department further says he resides in Rochester, Monroe Co. N.Y.
And his Post Office address is Rochester, Monroe Co. N.Y.
He makes this declaration in order to obtain the pension which he is entitled by virtue of his service and the
disability aforesaid under the Act of Congress approved July 14th 1862. And he hereby constitutes and appoints
Stan Benidict of Rochester, N.Y. his true and lawful Attorney with full power of substitution, to prosecute this his claim and to receive and receipt for any certificate, draft or money which may be due
to this deponent.

             Wm H. Skinner

Also personally appeared   Wm. H. Skinner Jr. and   James E. Bowman
residents of the City of Rochester in the County of Monroe
in said State of New York. Persons whom I certify to be respectable and entitled to credit and who being by me
duly sworn say that they were present and saw William H. Skinner Sr. further swear his name
to the forgoing declaration and they have every reason to believe, from the appearance
of the applicant and their acquaintance with him, that he is the identical person he represents himself to be
and they further state that they have no interest in the prosecution of this claim.

             Wm H. Skinner Sr.
             James E. Bowman

Subscribed and Sworn to before me by said   William H. Skinner

       The said declaim and by   William H. Skinner Sr.
       and   James E. Bowman   the said witness
       respectively this 20 day of January
         1866.   And I certify that I have no interest direct or indirect in the
         prosecution of this claim.
     In Testimony Whereof, Witness my hand and seal of said City and
     County at Rochester, N. Y. this 20 day
     of January 1866.

           J. _____?_____   Clerk

APPLICATION FOR INVALID PENSION.

State of New York,
COUNTY OF Monroe } ss.

On this 20th day of January A.D. one thousand eight hundred and sixty six personally appeared before me Clerk of the Monroe County Court, within and for the County and State aforesaid William H. Skinner aged 24 years, a resident of Rochester in the County of Monroe in the State of New York, who being duly sworn according to law, declares that he is the identical William H. Skinner who enlisted in the service of the United States at Rochester N.Y. on the eighth day of August in the year 1862 was a Private in Company F commanded by Captain D. E. Pierce in the 108th Regiment of New York Volunteers in the war of 1861, and was honorably discharged at Douglass Hospital in the State of Columbia on the fifteenth day of August A.D. 1865; that while in the service of the United States, and in the line of his duty he received the following wound viz. That while in the U.S. service and in the line of his duty, he was wounded by a shell fired by the enemy at the battle of Gettysburg Pa. on the third day of July 1863. Said shell struck him in the thigh of the left leg carrying away part of the leg and injuring the cords and muscles. Said wound immediately disabled him for duty, he was carried back to Field Hospital and from there to Jarvis Hospital Baltimore Md where he arrived the 14 of July 1863 and remained there nearly eleven months, during which time he was mostly confined to his bed. He was not able to straighten his leg and was all the time under the Surgeons charge. From there he was transferred to City Point Hospital where he remained until the 8th of Sept. 1864 when his wound again opened. He was then removed to Douglass Hospital Washington DC where he remained until he was discharged on the 15th day of August 1865. Before entering the army he worked on a farm but is now unable to resume that avocation on account of said wound. nor is he able to labor at any kind of work whatever. His wound troubles him so much that he can hardly walk.

Deponent further says he resides at Rochester Monroe Co. N.Y. and his Post Office address is Rochester Monroe Co. N.Y.

He makes this declaration in order to obtain the pension to which he is entitled by virtue of his service and the disability aforesaid, under the Act of Congress approved July 14th, 1862. And he hereby constitutes and appoints Starr H Benedict of Rochester N.Y. his true and lawful Attorney, with full power of substitution, to prosecute this his claim and to receive and receipt for any certificate, draft or money which may be due to this deponent.

Wm H. Skinner

Also, personally appeared Wm H Skinner Sr and James E Bowman residents of the city of Rochester in the County of Monroe in said State of New York, persons whom I certify to be respectable, and entitled to credit, and who, being by me duly sworn, say that they were present, and saw William H. Skinner sign his name to the foregoing declaration; and they further swear that they have every reason to believe, from the appearance of the applicant and their acquaintance with him, that he is the identical person he represents himself to be, and they further state that they have no interest in the prosecution of this claim.

Wm H Skinner Sr
James E Bowman

SUBSCRIBED AND SWORN to before me, by said the said declarant, and by William H Skinner and William H Skinner Sr and James E Bowman the said witnesses respectively this 20 day of January 1866. And I certify that I have no interest, direct or indirect, in the prosecution of this claim.

In Testimony Whereof Witness my hand and seal of said Court and of said County, at Rochester N.Y. this 20 day of January 1866.

A. Butterby, Clerk.

Pension request ... February 10th 1866

State of New York
County of Monroe

On this 10th day of February A. D. 1866 before the undersigned appeared Samuel Porter who being duly sworn says that William H. Skinner late a private in Co. "F" 108 Regiment New York Volunteers was wounded on the third day of July 1863 at the battle of Gettysburg Pa. by a shell fired by the enemy which struck him in the left thigh, injuring the cords and muscles and carrying part of the flesh. Said wound immediately disabled him from duty and he was carried back to a field hospital in the rear. That at the time said wound was received he was in the service of the United States, and in the line of duty – I also certify that I was Captain of Co. "F" of the 108th Regiment New York Volunteers, duly commissioned as such under whom he served at that time, and that this certificate is made from my private knowledge of the facts as above stated having been present at the battle said Skinner was wounded, and at the request of said William H. Skinner and in accordance with the regulating requirements of the Pension Office to enable him to receive an invalid pension, and that I have no pecuniary interest whatever in making this statement.

Samuel Porter
Late Capt. 108th N. Y.

Sworn and subscribed before me, this 10th day of Feb'y A. D. 1866 at Rochester N. Y. and certify that I have no interest in the claim.

A. J. Wilkins
Com. of Deeds

State of New York }
County of Monroe } ss.

On this 10th day of February A.D. 1866 before the undersigned appeared Samuel Porter who being duly sworn says. That William N. Skinner late a Private in Co. "F" 108 Regiment New York Volunteers was wounded on the 3rd day of July 1863 at the battle of Gettysburgh N.Y. by a shell fired by the enemy which struck him in the left thigh, injuring the cords and muscles and carrying part of the flesh. Said wound immediately disabled him from duty and he was carried back to a Field Hospital in the rear. That at the time said wound was received he was in the service of the United States and in the line of his duty— I also certify that I was Captain of Co. "F" of the 108th Regiment New York Volunteers, duly commissioned as such, under whom he served at that time, & that this Certificate is made from my Positive knowledge of the facts as above stated having been present at the battle said Skinner was wounded, & at the request of said William N. Skinner and in accordance with the regulations & requirements of the Pension Office to enable him to secure an Invalid Pension. & that I have no pecuniary interest whatever in making this statement.

Saml Porter
Late Capt 108th N.Y.

Sworn to & Subscribed before me, this 10th day of Feby A.D. 1866 at Rochester N.Y.
& I certify that I have no interest in the claim.

A. J. Wilkin
Court Stewd

EXAMINING SURGEON'S CERTIFICATE.

<u>Rochester N. Y. Feb.. 9. 1867</u>

I hereby certify, that I have carefully examined <u>**William H. Skinner**</u>, late a <u>**private Co. "F"**</u> <u>**108* Regiment New York Vols.**</u> in the service of the United States, who was discharged at <u>**Washington D. C.**</u>, on the <u>**16**</u> day of <u>**August**</u>, <u>1865</u>, and is an applicant for an invalid pension, by reason of alleged disability resulting from <u>**gun shot & Hernia**</u>

In my opinion the said <u>**Wm. H. Skinner**</u> is, <u>**one third**</u> incapacitated for obtaining his subsistence by manual labor from the cause above noted. <u>**The Hernia**</u>

Judging from his present condition, and from the evidence before me, it is my belief that the said disability <u>**may have been contracted**</u> in the service aforesaid in the line of duty.

The disability is <u>**uncertain deflation**</u>

A more particular description of the applicant's condition is subjoined:

<u>At Gettysburg Pa. he was wounded flesh wound</u>
<u>of left thigh. There is a large cicatrix - no utrophy.</u>
<u>He has a small Hernia which he states</u>
<u>he first noticed in hospital after he returned</u>
<u>from his regiment with his wound reopened -</u>
<u>He does not know when it appeared -</u>

H. F. Montgomery   *Examining Surgeon.*

Examining Surgeon's Certificate.

Rochester N.Y. Feb. 9, 1867.

I hereby certify, That I have carefully examined William H. Skinner, late a Private Co "F" 108 Regiment New York Vols.

Applicant's service.

in the service of the United States, who was discharged at Washington D.C., on the 16 day of August, 1865, and is an applicant for an invalid pension, by reason of alleged disability resulting from Gunshot & Hernia

In my opinion the said Wm. H. Skinner

Degree of disability.

is One Third incapacitated for obtaining his subsistence by manual labor from the cause above stated. The Hernia

Origin.

Judging from his present condition, and from the evidence before me, it is my belief that the said disability may have been contracted in the service aforesaid in the line of duty.

Probable duration.

The disability is uncertain duration

A more particular description of the applicant's condition is subjoined:

Particular description.

At Gettysburg Pa. he was wounded flesh wound of left thigh. There is a large cicatrix. No atrophy. He has a small inguinal Hernia which he states he first noticed in hospital after he returned from his regiment with his wound reopened — He does not know when it appeared —

Ordered

H. F. Montgomery
Examining Surgeon.

ACT OF JULY 14, 1862.
WAR OF 1861.

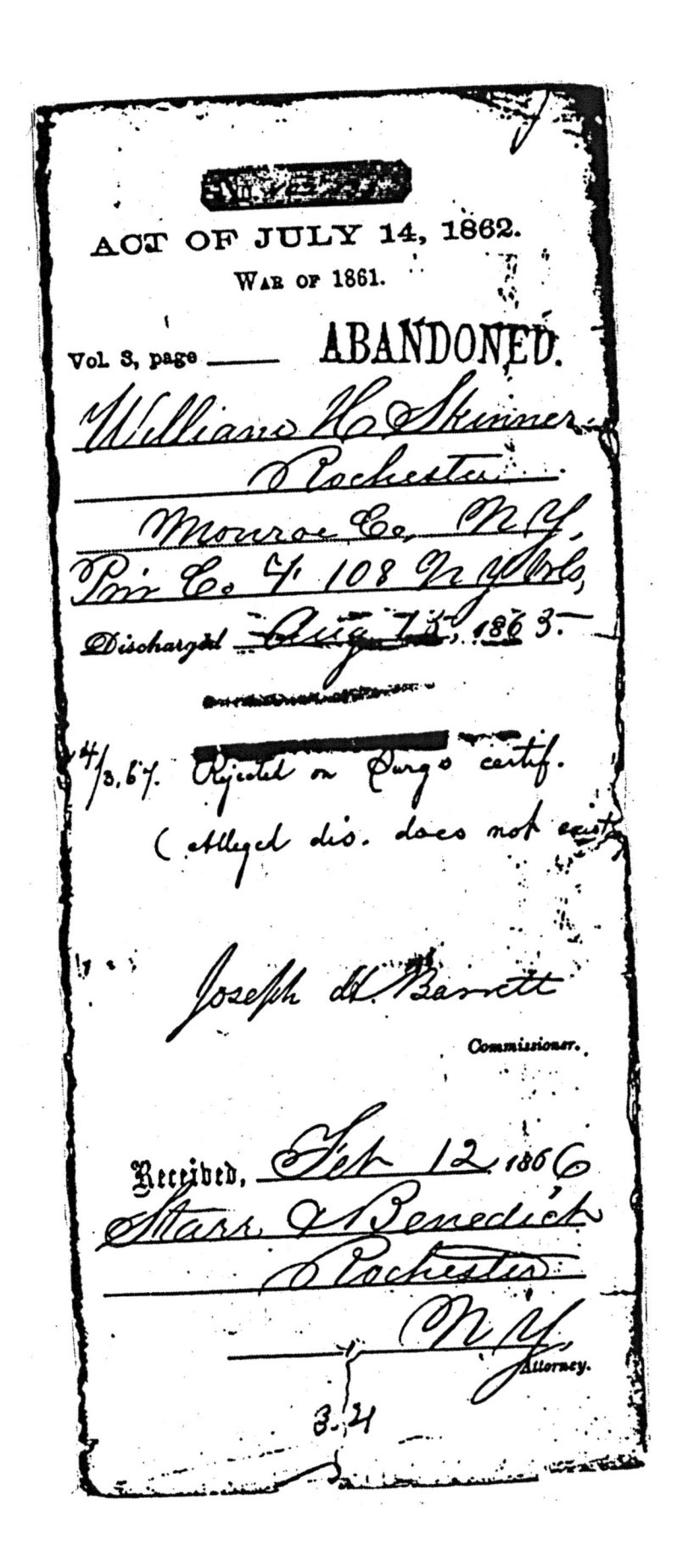

Vol. 3, page ____ **ABANDONED.**

William H. Skinner
Rochester
Monroe Co., N.Y.
Priv. Co. F, 108 N.Y. Vols.
Discharged Aug. 15, 1863.

4/3.67. Rejected on Surg's certif.
(Alleged dis. does not exist)

Joseph W. Barrett
Commissioner.

Received, Feb. 12, 1866
Starr & Benedict
Rochester
N.Y.
Attorney.

3.31

Letter to Lucy ... January 29th 1968

Manistee, Jan. 29th 68

Dear Lucy,

Your letter arrived in due time and I was very glad to get it; should have answered sooner, but have been delaying with the hope that someone would compel me to it as Mother did you. Am very sorry indeed that compulsion is necessary; but we will drop that, for we both are aware that quarreling is entirely out of place with us. Your letter was very welcome I assure you, as they always have been, not withstanding your predictions to the contrary.

You say I don't love you any longer! Mother and Father think the same! You jump at conclusions to hastily – ditto Mother and Father. I assure you I have the same feelings for you all that I always had.

You intimated as much as that you were going to be married soon! Why could you not trust me with the name of the man I may call brother some day?

Have you grown so tired of your own nearest relatives that you are so anxious to leave the country? Don't blame you for taking unto yourself a husband; expected such would be the case sometime, but object to your anticipating the day when you will leave them perhaps forever. You know tis different in my case! A man is not expected to remain at home all his days. You were indeed fortunate in the Christmas line. Your big brother

Hamilton Jan. 29" 18.

Dear Lucy;
Your letter arrived in due time and I was very glad to get it; I should have answered it sooner; but have been delaying with the hope that someone would come out to us as Mother did you. I am very sorry indeed that confusion be necessary but we will drop that; for we both are aware that quarreling is entirely out of place with me. Your letter was very welcome I assure you, as they always have been, notwithstanding your protestations to the contrary.

You say I don't love you any longer.! Mother and Father think so hardly - ditto Mother and Father. I assure you I have the same feelings for you all that I always had. You intimated or mentioned or that you were going to be married soon! (Why told you not trust me with the name of the man I may call Brother some day? Have you grown tired of your now meanest relations that you are so anxious to leave the country? Don't blame you for taking unto yourself a husband; expected such would be the case some time; but object to you anticipating the day so far, you will lean thereafter perhaps forever. You know its different on my own. A Man is not expected to remain at home all his days. You never endured privation in the Christmas time. (Our boy brothers.)

Letter to Lucy ... January 29th 1868

got nothing but a good dinner, that I am bound to have; have not been particularly lucky as far as making money is concerned, but take good care to get what I want to eat and not go ragged. Should have sent Mother what is her due if I had not had such confounded luck. But I will come out right side up with care one of these days. Am very sorry Lucy, that anyone was so unprincipled as to throw my misdemeanors up to you or any of the family. But Lucy, one thing to bear in mind, I am not so much to blame as you all imagine. There is one other more to blame that I.

Received Mother's letter with the key and _____ for trunk. The trunk has not arrived yet, expect it very soon now. Soon as it come I am off for a wormer climate. Am very sorry for Father; I hope he will be well soon. I am afraid that quinsy will not be got ride of so easily one of these days. My health has been good as usual.

You might have told me where you thought of going, so I could write to you.

Well Lucy good bye for a while I may drop in on you some day after you get domesticated.

Your Brother Will

got nothing but a good degree;
that I am bound to have. I have
not been particularly lucky as far as making
money is concerned, but take good care to
get what I want to eat and not go ragged. I
should have put Mother what she has done
if I had not had such confounded luck.
But I will come out right side up with care
one of these days. Am very sorry that
any one was so improper & ill tempered
(medsome up hig) in any of the family
But Lucy, nothing can be avoided, I am
not so much to blame as you all imagine.
there is no other man to blame than I.
Received Mothers letter with the key
and $2. for trunk; the trunk has
not arrived yet, expect it any day and now
and as it is warm I am not for a warm
climate. Am very sorry for Gertie. I
hope she will be well soon. I am afraid
that Quincy will not be well rid of so
easily one of these days. My health
has been good as usual.

You might have told me when
you thought of going so I
could write to you.
Well Lucy good bye for a while
I may drop in on you some day after
you get domesticated.

Your Brother — Ulie
"

EPILOGUE

Will Skinner in his last letter to a member of his family (Lucy) was written Jan. 29, 1868 from Manistee a city in north west Michigan. He stated that he was going to live in a warmer climate.

Questions arise: Why was he in Manistee ?
Did the family ever hear from him again ?
Did he go to a warmer climate such as Charleston, NC ?
Did he stay in Manistee ?

My aunt gave me a death date of July 31, 1868 but there is no known record to support that date, location or how.

The family story passed on by my grandfather DeWitt Skinner (a younger brother of Will) and my father was that Will had gone south and was killed in a bar room brawl by some former Confederate soldiers. Possible ?

I have made some effort (without any success) to locate evidence of his life/death in the Charleston and Manistee area.

WHAT HAPPENED TO MY GREAT UNCLE, WILL SKINNER ? ? ?

With the publication of this book a man's life is officially layed to rest.

About the Author

Gordon J Skinner was born in 1915. Spent 4 1/2 years in a Tank Destroyer army unit in WWII, graduated from College in 1946, worked for 32 years at Eastman Kodak Co. where he had developed an apprentice training program and later retired as a Technical Writer.

Gord still has a great deal of interest in baseball, basketball and soccer - sports that he played throughout his school years, army life and at the YMCA.

Active participation in his Presbyterian Church has also been a large part of his life.

To contact the author email gordskin@frontiernet.net

Pictured is the author holding the Civil War rifle which had been carried by his great uncle.

This book may be purchased by calling AuthorHouse at 888.280.7715 or online at www.authorhouse.com.

Printed in the United States
92855LV00003B/111-210/A